P9-DBX-951

E*new*ntertaining

THE AUSTRALIAN
Women's Weekly

contents

The simple act of cooking a meal and sharing it with your loved ones is an age-old and truly genuine way to say you care for them. The trick is to be able to do it without any hassle, so it's a good experience for everyone and can happen often. This book has recipes for delicious mains, and suggestions for easy starters and desserts – a modern cook's guide to an impressive menu.

Pamela Clark

Food Director

'New entertaining' is a modern style of entertaining, borne out of tight schedules and hectic lifestyles

You want a sensational meal, but don't want to be stuck in the kitchen all day and night. To achieve this seemingly impossible task, we've included recipes for impressive main meals, and suggested starters and desserts from a selection of dishes that are either bought or simply assembled.

When planning your menu, start by choosing a main meal that is within your budget, caters for all your guests' dietary requirements, and can be prepared in the amount of time available to you. Then choose a starter that readies the tastebuds for what is to come and a dessert you can prepare in advance of the dinner or that is simply plated and served. If your main course is rich and heavy, choose a fresh, light starter and dessert to complement the flavours of the main without leaving your guests feeling ready to burst. For a stress-free weeknight meal, plan a menu with a quick-and-easy main and store-bought starter and dessert. These rules of thumb are the key to easy, modern entertaining and will let you enjoy both great food and the company of your loved ones.

Main Courses Seafood

Fish curry with corn & pumpkin

2 tablespoons peanut oil
1 large brown onion (200g), sliced thinly
¼ cup (75g) red curry paste
1⅔ cups (410ml) coconut milk
1 cup (250ml) fish stock
600g butternut pumpkin, cut into 2cm cubes
230g baby corn, halved lengthways
2 medium red capsicums (400g),
    chopped coarsely
6 x 180g white fish fillets, skin on
1 tablespoon fish sauce
2 tablespoons lime juice
2 teaspoons brown sugar
150g baby spinach leaves

1 Heat half the oil in large saucepan; cook onion, stirring, until softened. Add paste; cook, stirring, until fragrant.
2 Add coconut milk, stock, pumpkin, corn and capsicum, cover; cook over low heat, stirring occasionally, about 10 minutes or until vegetables are tender.
3 Meanwhile, heat remaining oil in large frying pan; cook fish, skin-side down, about 3 minutes or until skin is crisp; turn, cook until fish is cooked as desired.
4 Stir sauce, juice and sugar into vegetable mixture; stir in spinach. Divide curry among serving bowls; top each with two pieces of fish.
prep & cook time 40 minutes **serves** 6
nutritional count per serving 29.6g total fat (15.5g saturated fat); 2307kJ (552 cal); 22.8g carbohydrate; 45.3g protein; 7.4g fibre

serving idea Steamed jasmine rice, lime wedges and coriander leaves.
tips We used snapper in this recipe, but you can use any white fish fillets.
This is a last-minute curry. To save a little time, prepare the vegetables ahead.

Menu Suggestion
starter Fennel, pecan and parsley salad, page 102
dessert Honeyed bananas with lime, page 109

Pan-fried whiting with leek, tomato & olive salsa

1kg kipfler potatoes, chopped coarsely
¼ cup (60ml) olive oil
12 x 80g whiting fillets, skin on
¼ cup (35g) plain flour
leek, tomato and green olive salsa
2 tablespoons olive oil
2 medium leeks (700g), trimmed, sliced thinly
2 cloves garlic, crushed
500g cherry tomatoes, halved
150g seeded large green olives, quartered
1 cup firmly packed fresh flat-leaf parsley leaves

1 Make leek, tomato and green olive salsa.
2 Boil, steam or microwave potato until tender; drain. Place in large bowl, drizzle with 1 tablespoon of the oil; cover to keep warm.
3 Coat fish in flour, shake off any excess; heat remaining oil in large frying pan. Cook fish, skin-side down, in batches, until skin crisps; turn, cook until cooked through. Serve fish with potatoes and salsa.

leek, tomato and green olive salsa Heat oil in medium saucepan, add leek; cook, stirring occasionally, until tender. Add garlic; cook, stirring, until fragrant. Stir in tomato and olives; cook until heated through. Remove from heat; stir in parsley.

prep & cook time 30 minutes **serves** 6
nutritional count per serving 19.6g total fat (3.3g saturated fat); 2073kJ (496 cal); 36.3g carbohydrate; 39.5g protein; 7.9g fibre

Menu Suggestion
starter Crostini with fetta, artichokes and rocket, page 105
dessert Fresh peaches with lemon and mint, page 109

serving idea Steamed green beans.
tip Make the salsa up to a day ahead, except for the addition of the parsley – add it just before you start to cook.

Menu Suggestion
starter Beetroot dip with grissini and olives, page 98
dessert Middle-eastern tasting plate, page 110

Barbecued salmon with chermoulla sauce

6 x 180g salmon fillets, skin on
2 tablespoons olive oil
2 medium red onions (340g),
3 medium zucchini (360g), sliced thinly,
    lengthways
340g asparagus, trimmed
chermoulla sauce
½ cup firmly packed fresh flat-leaf
    parsley leaves
½ cup firmly packed fresh coriander leaves
2 cloves garlic, chopped coarsely
1 teaspoon chilli flakes
1 teaspoon ground cumin
1 teaspoon ground coriander
½ teaspoon ground turmeric
1 tablespoon lemon juice
1 tablespoon olive oil
½ cup (140g) greek-style yogurt

1 Make chermoulla sauce.
2 Rub fish skin with a little of the oil.
3 Cut each onion into 8 wedges, keeping root ends intact. Combine onion, zucchini and asparagus with remaining oil in medium bowl.
4 Cook fish on heated barbecue flat plate, skin-side down, until skin crisps; turn, cook as desired. Cook vegetables on barbecue at the same time as the fish until tender. Serve fish and vegetables with sauce.

chermoulla sauce Blend or process herbs, garlic, chilli and ground spices until combined. Add juice and oil; process until smooth. Transfer to medium bowl; stir in yogurt.

prep & cook time 30 minutes **serves** 6
nutritional count per serving 23.8g total fat (5.2g saturated fat); 1701kJ (407 cal); 7.2g carbohydrate; 39.6g protein; 3.1g fibre

serving idea Steamed couscous.
tip Prepare the vegetables and the sauce up to a day ahead; keep the sauce, covered, in the refrigerator.

Oven-baked fish with lemon & mint risotto

1 litre (4 cups) vegetable stock
½ cup (125ml) water
20g butter
2 tablespoons olive oil
1 large brown onion (200g), chopped finely
1½ cups (300g) arborio rice
⅓ cup (80ml) dry white wine
6 x 180g white fish fillets, skin on
⅓ cup finely chopped fresh mint leaves
1 tablespoon fresh lemon thyme leaves
2 teaspoons finely grated lemon rind
2 tablespoons lemon juice
30g butter, extra
⅓ cup (25g) finely grated parmesan cheese

1 Place stock and the water in medium saucepan; bring to the boil. Reduce heat, simmer, covered.
2 Heat butter and half the oil in large heavy-based saucepan; cook onion, stirring, until soft. Add rice; stir to coat rice in onion mixture. Add wine; bring to the boil. Reduce heat; simmer, stirring, until liquid is almost evaporated.
3 Stir 1 cup of the simmering stock mixture into rice mixture; cook, stirring, over low heat, until liquid is absorbed. Continue adding stock mixture in 1 cup batches, stirring until absorbed after each addition. Total cooking time will be about 35 minutes or until rice is tender.
4 Meanwhile, preheat oven to 180°C/160°C fan-forced. Line oven tray with baking paper.
5 About 10 minutes before risotto is cooked, heat remaining oil in large frying pan. Brown fish, skin-side down, until skin crisps; turn, cook 1 minute. Transfer fillets to oven tray, skin-side up. Cook in oven about 7 minutes.
6 Stir herbs, rind, juice, extra butter and cheese into risotto. Serve fish with risotto; garnish with a little more chopped butter, finely sliced lemon rind and extra lemon thyme leaves.

prep & cook time 40 minutes **serves** 6
nutritional count per serving 20.3g total fat (8.6g saturated fat); 1910kJ (457 cal); 42.9g carbohydrate; 44.9g protein; 1.1g fibre

tip We used barramundi in this recipe, but you can use any white fish fillets. The most time-consuming part of making this risotto is the stirring. Have the ingredients ready to add and involve your guests, even if it's sharing a chat and a glass of wine as you stir.

Menu Suggestion
starter Warm orange and fennel olives, page 105
dessert Affogato with frangelico, page 106

Menu Suggestion
starter Pear and witlof salad, page 105
dessert Roasted blueberries with brie, page 110

Seafood stew with fennel

2 baby fennel bulbs (260g)
2 tablespoons lemon juice
1 tablespoon olive oil
2 medium brown onions (300g),
   chopped finely
4 cloves garlic, crushed
1 orange
⅓ cup (80ml) dry white wine
1 teaspoon chilli flakes
pinch saffron threads
2 x 400g cans diced tomatoes
1 litre (4 cups) fish stock
1 teaspoon white sugar
800g uncooked medium king prawns
800g small black mussels
750g skinless white fish fillets,
   cut into 3cm pieces

garlic croûtons
675g loaf sourdough bread, sliced thickly
3 cloves garlic, halved
2 tablespoons olive oil

1 Trim fennel; reserve fronds. Slice fennel as thinly as possible; combine with lemon juice in small bowl.
2 Heat oil in large saucepan; cook onion, stirring, until soft. Add garlic; cook, stirring, 1 minute.

3 Peel 3 thin strips of rind from orange. Stir rind, wine, chilli and saffron into onion mixture; cook, stirring, 2 minutes. Add undrained tomatoes; simmer, uncovered, about 10 minutes or until mixture thickens slightly. Add stock; simmer, uncovered, about 20 minutes or until liquid is reduced by about a quarter. Stir in sugar.
4 Shell and devein prawns. Scrub mussels, remove beards.
5 Add prawns, mussels and fish to tomato mixture. Cover; simmer, stirring occasionally, about 5 minutes or until prawns change in colour and mussels open (discard any that do not).
6 Meanwhile, make garlic croûtons.
7 Serve stew topped with fennel mixture and reserved fennel fronds; accompany with garlic croûtons.

garlic croûtons Toast bread both sides on heated grill plate (or grill or barbecue); rub one side of toast with cut garlic clove; drizzle with oil.

prep & cook time 1 hour **serves** 6
nutritional count per serving 17.2g total fat (3.5g saturated fat); 2792kJ (668 cal); 63.7g carbohydrate; 56.9g protein; 9.2g fibre

serving idea Mixed baby leaf salad.
tip You can buy the seafood already prepared from most fish markets; it will cost more, but will save you time.

Menu Suggestion
starter Fennel, pecan and parsley salad, page102
dessert Fresh peaches with lemon and mint, page 109

Seafood paella with aïoli

500g clams
½ teaspoon saffron threads
2 tablespoons boiling water
¼ cup (60ml) olive oil
1 large brown onion (200g), chopped finely
4 cloves garlic, crushed
4 medium tomatoes (600g) chopped finely
1 teaspoon white sugar
800g uncooked medium king prawns
2 teaspoons sweet paprika
1 litre (4 cups) water
2 cups (400g) arborio rice
400g skinless white fish fillets,
    cut into 4cm pieces
1 cup (120g) frozen peas
⅓ cup coarsely chopped fresh flat-leaf parsley
aïoli
1 cup (300g) mayonnaise
2 tablespoons lemon juice
2 cloves garlic, crushed

1 Rinse clams under cold water; place in large bowl of cold salted water, stand 2 hours. Discard water then rinse clams thoroughly; drain.
2 Combine saffron and the boiling water in small heatproof bowl.

3 Heat oil in 40cm-round shallow frying pan; cook onion over medium heat, stirring, about 10 minutes or until soft and golden brown. Add garlic; cook, stirring, 1 minute. Add tomato; cook, stirring frequently, about 15 minutes or until pulpy. Stir in sugar.
4 Meanwhile, shell and devein prawns, leaving tails intact.
5 Stir saffron mixture, paprika, the water and rice into pan; bring to the boil. Reduce heat, add clams, prawns and fish; simmer, uncovered, without stirring, about 20 minutes or until rice is almost tender. Sprinkle peas into pan; simmer, uncovered, about 3 minutes until liquid is absorbed. Remove pan from heat, cover; stand 10 minutes. Stir in parsley.
6 Meanwhile, make aïoli. Serve paella with aïoli.
aïoli Combine ingredients in small serving bowl.
prep & cook time 1 hour (+ standing)
serves 6
nutritional count per serving 28.2g total fat (4g saturated fat); 2897kJ (693 cal); 68.9g carbohydrate; 38.2g protein; 4.3g fibre

serving idea Mesclun salad.
tips Bomba or calasparra are the correct Spanish rices to use for paella, but arborio (a short-grain white) rice will do just as well. Prepare the seafood and aïoli ahead of time. Some fish markets sell prepared clams, shelled prawns and chopped chunks of fish – buy these if you're short on time.

Menu Suggestion
starter Pear and witlof salad, page 105
dessert A platter of sliced melons

Singapore chilli crab

4 x 325g uncooked blue swimmer crabs
2 tablespoons peanut oil
3 cloves garlic, chopped finely
4cm piece fresh ginger (20g), grated
1 fresh small red thai chilli, sliced thinly
⅓ cup (85ml) bottled tomato pasta sauce
2 tablespoons chilli sauce
2 tablespoons japanese soy sauce
⅓ cup (80ml) water
2 teaspoons white sugar
½ cup firmly packed fresh coriander leaves

1 Lift flap under body of each crab; turn crab over, hold body with one hand while pulling off top part of shell with the other. Discard shell and gills on either side of body. Rinse crab under cold water; chop body into quarters.
2 Heat oil in wok; stir-fry garlic, ginger and chilli; stir-fry until fragrant. Add sauces, the water and sugar; stir-fry 2 minutes.
3 Add crab; cook, covered, over medium heat, about 10 minutes or until crab has changed colour. Serve sprinkled with coriander.
prep & cook time 30 minutes **serves** 4
nutritional count per serving 10.1g total fat (1.8g saturated fat); 723kJ (173 cal); 8.2g carbohydrate; 11.6g protein; 1.6g fibre

serving idea Steamed jasmine rice and baby asian salad greens.
tips Most fish markets that sell uncooked crustaceans will prepare them for you – ready for cooking – so the rest of the recipe is easy. You'll need a large wok for efficient cooking. We've used blue swimmer crab, but any fresh crab can be used.

Baked whole fish with celery & walnut salad

1.8kg cleaned whole white fish
1 lemon, sliced thinly
600g spring onions, trimmed, halved
2 tablespoons olive oil
¼ cup (60ml) dry white wine

celery & walnut salad
2 bunches red radishes (500g), trimmed, sliced thinly
3 stalks celery (450g), trimmed, sliced thinly
1 small red onion (100g), halved, sliced thinly
1 cup (110g) coarsely chopped roasted walnuts
1 cup firmly packed fresh coriander leaves
¼ cup (60ml) olive oil
2 tablespoons red wine vinegar
2 teaspoons dijon mustard
½ teaspoon brown sugar

1 Preheat oven to 200°C/180°C fan-forced.
2 Pat fish dry inside and out with absorbent paper. Score fish four times both sides. Place lemon inside cavity.
3 Place onions lengthways in large shallow baking dish; place fish on onions; drizzle with combined oil and wine. Cook fish, uncovered, about 30 minutes.
4 Meanwhile, make celery & walnut salad.
5 Serve fish with salad.

celery & walnut salad Combine radish, celery, onion, nuts and coriander in medium bowl. Combine oil, vinegar, mustard and sugar in a screw-top jar; shake well. Drizzle over salad.

prep & cook time 40 minutes **serves** 6
nutritional count per serving 32.8g total fat (4.7g saturated fat); 2077kJ (497 cal); 8.2g carbohydrate; 38.7g protein; 5.9g fibre

serving idea Sprinkle with micro-cress leaves, and serve with a loaf of warm crusty bread.
tips We used whole pink snapper in this recipe, but you can use any whole white fish. Micro-cress is cress that has been harvested at seedling stage. It has small, tender, green leaves with a strong radish-like flavour. It is available year-round in specialty grocers. If you can't find any, use baby salad greens, instead.

Menu Suggestion
starter Pitta crisps with eggplant dip, page 98
dessert Turkish delight sundae, page 106

Main Courses Poultry

Roasted lemon & herb chicken

3 x 500g small chickens
1kg pontiac potatoes, cut into 2cm-thick slices
2 tablespoons olive oil
3 lemons, cut into wedges
2 tablespoons fresh thyme sprigs
2 tablespoons fresh oregano leaves
¾ cup (180ml) dry white wine
¼ cup (50g) rinsed, drained baby capers

1 Preheat oven to 220°C/200°C fan-forced.
2 Rinse chickens under cold water; pat dry with absorbent paper. Using kitchen scissors, cut along chickens' backbones; discard backbones. Cut chickens in half; place chicken, skin-side up, and potato, in single layer, on 2 large shallow baking dishes. Drizzle with oil. Squeeze juice from one lemon over chicken, add remaining wedges to dishes; sprinkle with herbs.
3 Roast, uncovered, 50 minutes. Add wine and capers to dishes; roast, uncovered, about 10 minutes or until chickens are cooked. Sprinkle with extra fresh oregano leaves before taking to the table, if you like.
prep & cook time 1¼ hours **serves** 6
nutritional count per serving 26.5g total fat (7.1g saturated fat); 1944kJ (465 cal); 21.2g carbohydrate; 28.9g protein; 4.5g fibre

serving idea Mixed leaf salad.
tips The roasted lemon wedges are meant to be eaten; during cooking their tartness mellows, making them lusciously delicious. Leave the potatoes unpeeled, if you like; just give them a good scrub before slicing.

Menu Suggestion
starter Fennel, pecan and parsley salad, page 102
dessert Chocolate ice-cream with toffee-brittle, page 110

Roast duck with orange and snow pea salad

4 medium oranges (960g)
½ cup (125ml) oyster sauce
½ cup (125ml) chinese cooking wine
¼ cup (55g) brown sugar
6 star anise
6 x 150g duck breast fillets
2 teaspoons peanut oil
2 teaspoons sesame oil
300g snow peas, trimmed, sliced thinly
150g baby spinach leaves
1 small red onion (100g), sliced thinly
2 teaspoons sesame seeds, toasted

1 Peel 4 thin strips of rind from one of the oranges. Juice this orange (you need ¼ cup juice); refrigerate.
2 Combine rind in small saucepan with sauce, cooking wine, sugar and star anise; stir over heat until sugar dissolves. Bring marinade to the boil; remove from heat, cool.
3 Combine marinade with duck in large bowl. Cover; refrigerate 3 hours or overnight.
4 Preheat oven to 220°C/200°C fan-forced. Line oven tray with baking paper.
5 Drain duck; reserve marinade. Heat peanut oil in large frying pan; cook duck, skin-side down, over high heat about 1 minute or until skin is golden brown. Turn duck; cook 1 minute. Place duck, skin-side up, on tray; roast, uncovered, in oven, about 10 minutes or until cooked as desired. Stand duck 5 minutes.
6 Meanwhile, combine ¼ cup of the reserved marinade with 1 tablespoon water in small saucepan; bring to the boil. Reduce heat; simmer, uncovered, 5 minutes. Whisk in orange juice and sesame oil.
7 Segment remaining oranges into medium bowl; add peas, spinach and onion to bowl; mix gently. Divide salad among plates; top with sliced duck, drizzle with warm dressing then sprinkle with sesame seeds.

prep & cook time 35 minutes (+ refrigeration)
serves 6
nutritional count per serving 59.5g total fat (17.3g saturated fat); 3143kJ (752 cal); 26.9g carbohydrate; 23.9g protein; 4.3g fibre

tips It's well worth marinating the duck breasts overnight. Using both the stove top and the oven will result in perfectly cooked duck.

Menu Suggestion
starter Oysters with mirin and cucumber, page 102
dessert Plums with creamy vanilla yogurt, page 113

Pomegranate and burghul chicken salad

¼ cup (60ml) olive oil
¼ cup (60ml) pomegranate molasses
1 tablespoon ground cumin
2 cloves garlic, crushed
1kg chicken breast fillets
1½ cups (375ml) chicken stock
1½ cups (240g) burghul
1 cup (250ml) pomegranate pulp
1 medium red onion (170g), sliced thinly
350g watercress, trimmed
2 cups firmly packed fresh
    flat-leaf parsley leaves
1 cup (110g) coarsely chopped roasted walnuts
150g piece fetta cheese, crumbled
pomegranate dressing
¼ cup (60ml) olive oil
¼ cup (60ml) lemon juice
3 teaspoons honey
3 teaspoons pomegranate molasses

1 Combine oil, molasses, cumin and garlic in large bowl with chicken. Cover; refrigerate 3 hours or overnight.
2 Bring stock to the boil in medium saucepan. Remove from heat, add burghul; cover, stand 5 minutes.
3 Meanwhile, make pomegranate dressing.

4 Drain chicken, discard marinade. Cook chicken on heated oiled grill plate (or grill or barbecue), until browned both sides and cooked through. Cover chicken; stand 10 minutes then slice thickly.
5 Combine chicken, burghul and remaining ingredients with dressing in large bowl; divide among serving plates.
pomegranate dressing Combine ingredients in screw-top jar; shake well.
prep & cook time 45 minutes (+ refrigeration)
serves 6
nutritional count per serving 47.1g total fat (10.3g saturated fat); 3503kJ (838 cal); 47.6g carbohydrate; 50.2g protein; 13.1g fibre

---

tips You need one large pomegranate to get the amount of pulp required for this recipe. To remove the pulp from the pomegranate, cut it in half, then hit the skin of the halves with a wooden spoon – the seeds usually fall out easily. Pomegranate molasses is available at Middle-Eastern food stores, specialty food shops and some delicatessens.
If you're short of time, it's fine to skip the marinating, just make sure the chicken is well-coated with the oil mixture.

Menu Suggestion
starter Beetroot dip with grissini and olives, page 98
dessert Middle-eastern tasting plate, page 110

Vermicelli noodle and chicken salad

2 litres (8 cups) water
800g chicken breast fillets
200g vermicelli noodles
150g snow peas, trimmed
8 green onions
2 medium carrots (240g)
½ medium wombok (500g), shredded finely
2 cups (160g) bean sprouts
1 cup firmly packed fresh mint leaves
1 cup firmly packed fresh coriander leaves
½ cup (70g) roasted unsalted peanuts,
    chopped coarsely

sweet chilli dressing
½ cup (125ml) lime juice
2 tablespoons fish sauce
3 teaspoons sambal oelek
2 teaspoons sesame oil
1 tablespoon brown sugar
1 clove garlic, crushed

1 Bring the water to the boil in large saucepan; add chicken. Simmer, uncovered, about 10 minutes or until chicken is cooked. Cool chicken in poaching liquid 10 minutes; drain. Using two forks, shred chicken coarsely.
2 Place noodles in large heatproof bowl, cover with boiling water; stand until tender, drain. Rinse under cold water, drain.
3 Meanwhile, make sweet chilli dressing.
4 Slice snow peas and onions diagonally into thin strips. Halve carrots crossways; cut into matchsticks. Combine peas, onion, carrot, wombok, sprouts, herbs and chicken in large bowl with noodles; drizzle with dressing. Serve salad sprinkled with nuts.

sweet chilli dressing Combine ingredients in screw-top jar; shake well.

prep & cook time 40 minutes **serves** 6
nutritional count per serving 15.1g total fat (3.1g saturated fat); 1772kJ (424 cal); 30.9g carbohydrate; 37.7g protein; 6.4g fibre

tip You can poach, shred and refrigerate the chicken a day ahead, and you can prepare the dressing and salad vegetables a day ahead. Keep them refrigerated then simply combine with the noodles when you're ready. Or, poach and shred the chicken, and use it warm with the salad ingredients and noodles.

Menu Suggestion
starter Pitta crisps with eggplant dip, page 98
dessert Honeyed bananas with lime, page 109

Menu Suggestion
starter Samosas with tamarind sauce, page 101
dessert Fresh peaches with lemon and mint, page 109

Hot & spicy chicken curry

¼ cup (60ml) vegetable oil
1.8kg chicken thigh fillets, halved
1 large brown onion (200g), sliced thinly
4 cloves garlic, crushed
3cm piece fresh ginger (15g), grated
10 curry leaves
400g can diced tomatoes
1 cup (250ml) chicken stock
10cm stick fresh lemon grass (20g), bruised
½ cup (125ml) coconut milk
1 cup loosely packed fresh coriander leaves

spice blend

1 tablespoon ground coriander
2 teaspoons ground cumin
1½ teaspoons ground turmeric
1 teaspoon ground cinnamon
1 teaspoon hot chilli powder
½ teaspoon ground fennel
½ teaspoon ground cardamom
½ teaspoon ground white pepper

1 Make spice blend.
2 Heat 2 tablespoons of the oil in large saucepan; cook chicken, in batches, until browned all over.
3 Heat remaining oil in same pan; cook onion, stirring, until soft. Add garlic, ginger and curry leaves; cook, stirring, until fragrant. Add spice blend; cook, stirring, about 2 minutes or until fragrant.
4 Stir chicken, undrained tomatoes, stock and lemon grass into pan; bring to the boil. Reduce heat; simmer, covered, stirring occasionally, 20 minutes. Uncover; simmer about 10 minutes or until sauce thickens slightly. Discard lemon grass.
5 Add coconut milk; stir until heated through. Serve curry sprinkled with coriander.

spice blend Combine spices in small bowl.
prep & cook time 1 hour **serves** 6
nutritional count per serving 35.5g total fat (11.6g saturated fat); 2399kJ (574 cal); 5.5g carbohydrate; 58g protein; 2.2g fibre

serving idea Steamed basmati rice.
tip This is a quick and easy curry – to save some time, make the spice blend well in advance. Put it in an airtight jar and store it in a dark place.

Menu Suggestion

starter Pâté with port onion jam, page 101
dessert Affogato with frangelico, page 106

Creamy mushroom, leek and chicken casserole

2 tablespoons olive oil
1.5kg chicken thigh fillets, quartered
3 rindless bacon rashers (195g),
    chopped coarsely
40g butter
3 medium leeks (1kg), trimmed, sliced thinly
3 stalks celery (450g), trimmed, sliced thinly
3 cloves garlic, crushed
¼ cup loosely packed fresh thyme sprigs
2 bay leaves
2 tablespoons plain flour
1½ cups (375ml) dry white wine
1½ cups (375ml) chicken stock
400g button mushrooms
¼ cup (60ml) cream
½ cup coarsely chopped fresh flat-leaf parsley

1 Preheat oven to 160°C/140°C fan-forced.
2 Heat oil in large heavy-based flameproof dish. Cook chicken, in batches, until browned all over.
3 Cook bacon, stirring, in same dish until browned lightly.
4 Add butter and leek; cook, stirring occasionally, until leek softens. Stir in celery, garlic, thyme and bay leaves. Stir in flour, then wine and stock; bring to the boil, stirring.
5 Stir in chicken and mushrooms; transfer to oven. Cook about 20 minutes or until chicken is cooked through and sauce has thickened slightly.
6 Return dish to stove top, discard bay leaves; stir in cream and parsley. Simmer, uncovered, until casserole is heated through. Garnish with fresh thyme leaves.

prep & cook time 50 minutes **serves** 6
nutritional count per serving 39.2g total fat (14.6g saturated fat); 2805kJ (671 cal); 8.6g carbohydrate; 59.1g protein; 6.2g fibre

serving idea Accompany with crusty bread.
tip It's fine to cook the bacon and leek mixture the day before; put it in the fridge then proceed with the recipe on the day of serving.

Menu Suggestion
starter Dolmades with minted yogurt and olives, page 98
dessert Strawberries in rosewater syrup, page 113

Barbecued chicken with minted tomato salad

2 tablespoons lemon juice

1 tablespoon sumac

2 teaspoons finely chopped fresh oregano

2 tablespoons olive oil

6 x 200g chicken breast fillets

3 lemons, halved

3 large pitta bread (240g)

minted tomato salad

2 tablespoons lemon juice

2 tablespoons olive oil

500g grape tomatoes, halved

2 lebanese cucumbers (260g),
   cut into ribbons

1 cup firmly packed fresh
   flat-leaf parsley leaves

1 cup firmly packed fresh mint leaves

2 teaspoons finely chopped fresh oregano

8 green onions, sliced thinly

1 Combine juice, sumac, oregano and half the oil in large bowl with chicken. Cover; refrigerate 3 hours or overnight.

2 Make minted tomato salad

3 Cook chicken on barbecue (or grill or grill plate) until browned both sides and cooked through. Stand 5 minutes then slice thickly.

4 Cook lemon, cut-side down, about 3 minutes or until browned lightly. Brush bread, both sides, with remaining oil; brown lightly on barbecue, break into coarse pieces.

5 Combine salad and bread; serve with chicken and lemon.

minted tomato salad Whisk juice and oil in large serving bowl; add remaining ingredients, toss gently to combine.

prep & cook time 35 minutes (+ refrigeration)

serves 6

nutritional count per serving 24.4g total fat (5.2g saturated fat); 2199kJ (526 cal); 25.6g carbohydrate; 48.2g protein; 5.4g fibre

tips Marinate the chicken overnight, if you can, for the best flavour. Prepare the ingredients for the salad, but combine them just before serving.

Roast chicken with preserved lemon

¼ cup finely chopped preserved lemon rind
6 cloves garlic, crushed
1½ teaspoons ground ginger
1 teaspoon ground cumin
1 teaspoon sweet paprika
1 teaspoon chilli flakes
½ teaspoon ground turmeric
2 tablespoons olive oil
2.5kg chicken thigh cutlets
¼ teaspoon saffron threads
1 cup (250ml) boiling water
4 medium brown onions (600g), sliced thinly
4 wide strips preserved lemon rind
150g drained green olives
1 cup loosely packed fresh coriander leaves

1 Combine chopped lemon rind, garlic, spices and half the oil in large bowl with chicken. Cover; refrigerate 3 hours or overnight.
2 Preheat oven to 180°C/160°C fan-forced.
3 Combine saffron and the water in small heatproof bowl.
4 Heat remaining oil in large frying pan; cook chicken, in batches, until browned both sides.

5 Add onion to pan; cook about 5 minutes or until softened. Add saffron mixture to pan; bring to the boil. Spread onion mixture into large shallow baking dish; add chicken, in single layer. Roast, uncovered, in oven 20 minutes.
6 Sprinkle lemon rind strips and olives over chicken; roast, uncovered, about 25 minutes or until cooked through.
7 Serve chicken sprinkled with coriander.
prep & cook time 1½ hours (+ refrigeration)
serves 6
nutritional count per serving 27.5g total fat (7.3g saturated fat); 2190kJ (524 cal); 11.9g carbohydrate; 56.3g protein; 2.8g fibre

serving idea Steamed couscous combined with sliced red onion, parsley and roasted blanched almonds.
tips Cut away and discard the flesh from the preserved lemon; rinse and drain the rind before using.
We used brine-cured sicilian olives in this recipe for their lovely flavour and texture. Crack them open but leave the seeds in; use the flat blade of a knife to split the olives. Remember to warn your guests about the seeds before they start eating.

Menu Suggestion

starter Beetroot dip with grissini and olives, page 98
dessert Turkish delight sundae, page 106

Main Courses Beef

Beef rendang

1.5kg beef chuck steak, trimmed,
  cut into 3cm cubes
400ml can coconut milk
½ cup (125ml) water
10cm stick fresh lemon grass (20g), bruised
3 fresh kaffir lime leaves, torn
spice paste
2 medium red onions (340g), chopped coarsely
4 cloves garlic, chopped coarsely
5cm piece fresh ginger (25g), chopped coarsely
2 fresh long red chillies, chopped coarsely
3 teaspoons grated fresh galangal
3 teaspoons ground coriander
1½ teaspoons ground cumin
1 teaspoon ground turmeric
1 teaspoon salt

1 Blend or process spice paste ingredients until combined.
2 Combine paste in wok with beef, coconut milk, the water, lemon grass and lime leaves; bring to the boil. Reduce heat; simmer, covered, stirring occasionally, about 2 hours or until mixture thickens and beef is tender.
prep & cook time 2¼ hours **serves** 6
nutritional count per serving 25.2g total fat (16.9g saturated fat); 1952kJ (467 cal); 6.1g carbohydrate; 52.9g protein; 2.5g fibre

serving idea Steamed jasmine rice, accompanied by combined finely chopped cucumber and finely sliced fresh red chilli in rice vinegar.
tip You can make the curry a day or two before you need it.

Menu Suggestion
starter Pitta crisps with eggplant dip, page 98
dessert Plums with creamy vanilla yogurt, page 113

Menu Suggestion

starter Bruschetta with tomato, basil and capers, page 102
dessert Great coffee with panforte, page 113

Osso buco

6 pieces veal osso buco (1.8kg)
½ cup (75g) plain flour
40g butter
2 tablespoons olive oil
3 stalks celery (450g), trimmed,
    chopped coarsely
6 drained anchovy fillets, chopped coarsely
¾ cup (180ml) dry white wine
2 x 400g cans diced tomatoes
½ cup (125ml) chicken stock
5 cloves garlic, crushed
3 bay leaves
10 fresh thyme sprigs
gremolata
½ cup finely chopped fresh flat-leaf parsley
2 cloves garlic, chopped finely
1 teaspoon finely grated lemon rind

1 Preheat oven to 160°C/140°C fan-forced.
2 Coat veal in flour, shake off any excess. Heat butter and oil in large frying pan; cook veal, in batches, until browned both sides. Transfer veal to large ovenproof dish.
3 Cook celery and anchovy in same pan, stirring, until celery softens. Add wine; bring to the boil. Stir in undrained tomatoes, stock, garlic, bay leaves and thyme; return to the boil.
4 Pour tomato mixture over veal. Cook, covered, in oven about 1½ hours or until veal starts to fall from the bone.
5 Meanwhile, make gremolata.
6 Serve osso buco sprinkled with gremolata.
gremolata Combine ingredients in small bowl.
prep & cook time 2 hours **serves** 6
nutritional count per serving 13.2g total fat (4.8g saturated fat); 1626kJ (389 cal); 14.4g carbohydrate; 46.1g protein; 3.8g fibre

serving idea Soft polenta.
tips Osso buco can be made a day or two ahead; keep covered in the refrigerator. Reheat, covered tightly, in the oven at 180°C/160°C fan-forced for about 1 hour.
Make and use the gremolata as close to serving time as possible.

Grilled steaks with anchovy butter and lemony potato wedges

6 x 220g new-york cut steaks
2 tablespoons olive oil
lemony potato wedges
1.5kg potatoes
¼ cup (60ml) olive oil
2 cloves garlic, crushed
1 tablespoon finely grated lemon rind
2 teaspoons sea salt flakes
anchovy butter
80g butter, softened
6 drained anchovy fillets, chopped coarsely
2 cloves garlic, crushed
2 tablespoons finely chopped fresh
 flat-leaf parsley

1 Make lemony potato wedges and anchovy butter.
2 About 10 minutes before wedges are cooked, brush beef all over with oil; cook on heated grill plate (or grill or barbecue) until cooked as desired. Cover beef; stand 5 minutes.
3 Serve beef topped with sliced anchovy butter and potato wedges.

lemony potato wedges Preheat oven to 220°C/200°C fan-forced. Line oven tray with baking paper. Slice potatoes lengthways into 8 wedges; boil, steam or microwave until slightly softened. Drain; pat dry with absorbent paper. Combine potato in large bowl with oil, garlic, rind and salt. Place wedges, in single layer, on tray; roast about 50 minutes or until browned lightly.

anchovy butter Mash ingredients in small bowl with fork until well combined. Roll mixture tightly in plastic wrap to make a log; refrigerate until firm.

prep & cook time 1 hour **serves** 6
nutritional count per serving 39.8g total fat (14.9g saturated fat); 2989kJ (715 cal); 33.1g carbohydrate; 53.7g protein; 5.5g fibre

serving idea Tossed green salad.
tips New-York cut steak is sometimes called boneless sirloin by butchers.
Make the anchovy butter a day, or even a month or so, ahead, if you like, and freeze it.

Menu Suggestion

starter Cheddar with spiced pear paste, page 101
dessert Chocolates with hot chocolate shots, page 109

Veal chops with caper sauce

1kg kipfler potatoes, halved lengthways
1 tablespoon olive oil
6 x 200g veal chops
20g butter
3 cloves garlic, crushed
½ cup (125ml) white grape verjuice
¼ cup (60ml) chicken stock
¼ cup (50g) rinsed, drained baby capers
¼ cup finely chopped fresh flat-leaf parsley
150g baby spinach leaves

1 Boil, steam or microwave potato until tender; drain. Cover to keep warm.
2 Meanwhile, heat oil in large frying pan; cook veal until cooked as desired. Cover veal; stand 5 minutes.
3 Melt butter in same pan; cook garlic, stirring, until fragrant. Add verjuice and stock to pan; bring to the boil, stirring until thickened slightly. Remove from heat; stir in capers and parsley.
4 Divide spinach and potato among serving plates; top with veal, spoon over sauce.

prep & cook time 30 minutes **serves** 6
nutritional count per serving 10g total fat (3.4g saturated fat); 1346kJ (322 cal); 22.8g carbohydrate; 33g protein; 3.8g fibre

tip Verjuice is unfermented grape juice with a fresh lemony-vinegar flavour. It's available in supermarkets, usually in the vinegar section.

Menu Suggestion

starter Crostini with fetta, artichokes and rocket, page 105
dessert Plums with creamy vanilla yogurt, page 113

Pepper steaks with mushroom sauce and creamy mash

2 tablespoons rinsed green peppercorns
in brine, drained, crushed
2 teaspoons cracked black pepper
6 x 150g beef fillet steaks
2 teaspoons olive oil
40g butter
400g swiss brown mushrooms, sliced thinly
½ cup (125ml) brandy
1½ cups (375ml) beef stock
300ml cream
2 tablespoons finely chopped fresh
flat-leaf parsley
creamy mash
1kg sebago potatoes, chopped coarsely
½ cup (125ml) hot milk
50g butter, chopped coarsely

1 Make creamy mash.
2 Combine peppers in small bowl; press all over beef. Heat oil in large frying pan; cook beef until cooked as desired. Cover to keep warm.
3 Melt butter in same pan; cook mushrooms, stirring, until tender. Add brandy; bring to the boil. Cook, stirring, until liquid has reduced slightly. Stir in stock and cream; cook, stirring, until sauce thickens slightly; stir in parsley.
4 Spoon sauce over beef; serve with mash.
creamy mash Boil, steam or microwave potato until tender; drain. Mash in large bowl with milk and butter. Cover to keep warm.

prep & cook time 30 minutes **serves** 6
nutritional count per serving 45.7g total fat (27g saturated fat); 2968kJ (710 cal); 22.7g carbohydrate; 40.1g protein; 4.2g fibre

serving idea Steamed sugar snap peas.
tips You can use either eye or scotch fillet for the recipe.
Use coarse cracked black pepper, not ground, as ground pepper will make the steaks too hot.
You can make the mash well ahead of serving; it will reheat well in a microwave oven.

Menu Suggestion
starter Pear and witlof salad, page 105
dessert Chocolate ice-cream with toffee-brittle, page 110

Menu Suggestion

starter Oysters with mirin and cucumber, page 102
dessert Fresh peaches with lemon and mint, page 109

Warm thai beef salad

800g piece beef rump steak
1 teaspoon peanut oil
250g bean thread vermicelli
1 telegraph cucumber (400g),
    halved lengthways, sliced thinly
1 large red capsicum (350g), sliced thinly
1 small red onion (100g), sliced thinly
1 fresh long red chilli, sliced thinly
1 cup firmly packed fresh mint leaves
1 cup firmly packed fresh coriander leaves

lime dressing

1 tablespoon coarsely chopped fresh
    coriander root and stem mixture
5 cloves garlic, chopped coarsely
1 teaspoon black peppercorns
½ cup (125ml) lime juice
1 tablespoon fish sauce
1 tablespoon grated palm sugar
2 x 10cm sticks fresh lemon grass (40g),
    chopped coarsely

1 Brush beef, both sides, with oil; cook on heated grill plate (or grill or barbecue) until cooked as desired. Cover beef; stand 5 minutes.
2 Place vermicelli in large heatproof bowl, cover with boiling water; stand until tender, drain. Cut vermicelli into random lengths into same bowl.
3 Meanwhile, make dressing.
4 Slice beef thinly; combine in large bowl with half the dressing and remaining ingredients. Drizzle remaining dressing over vermicelli. Divide vermicelli among shallow serving bowls; top with salad.
lime dressing Blend ingredients until chopped finely.

prep & cook time 30 minutes **serves** 6
nutritional count per serving 10.6g total fat (4.2g saturated fat); 1597kJ (382 cal); 34g carbohydrate; 35.3g protein; 3.4g fibre

tips The dressing can be made several hours ahead. The salad can be prepared leaving only the steak to cook and the vermicelli to soften.

starter Fig, prosciutto and antipasti salad, page 102
dessert Great coffee with panforte, page 113

Burgers italian-style

750g beef mince
1 medium red onion (170g), chopped finely
1 egg
1¼ cups (85g) stale breadcrumbs
½ cup (40g) finely grated parmesan cheese
⅓ cup finely chopped fresh flat-leaf parsley
1 clove garlic, crushed
1 teaspoon chilli flakes
3 medium red capsicums (600g)
1 tablespoon olive oil
12 slices ciabatta bread (420g)
150g drained marinated artichoke hearts,
    sliced thinly
60g rocket leaves
ripe tomato sauce
1 tablespoon olive oil
3 cloves garlic, sliced thinly
500g ripe small tomatoes, sliced thickly
2 teaspoons balsamic vinegar

1 Make ripe tomato sauce.
2 Meanwhile, combine beef, onion, egg, breadcrumbs, cheese, parsley, garlic and chilli flakes in medium bowl; shape mixture into six patties. Place patties on tray, cover; refrigerate until required.
3 Quarter capsicums; discard seeds and membranes. Roast under grill or in very hot oven, skin-side up, until skin blisters and blackens. Cover capsicum pieces with plastic or paper for 5 minutes; peel away skin then slice capsicum thinly.

4 Heat oil in large frying pan; cook patties, uncovered, about 5 minutes each side or until cooked through.
5 Preheat grill. Toast bread slices until golden. Spread half the bread slices with half the sauce; top with xartichoke, capsicum, patties, rocket then remaining sauce and remaining bread slices.
ripe tomato sauce Heat oil in medium saucepan; cook garlic, stirring, until fragrant. Add tomato; cook, uncovered, stirring occasionally, about 30 minutes or until sauce thickens slightly. Remove from heat; stir in vinegar.
prep & cook time 40 minutes (+ refrigeration)
serves 6
nutritional count per serving 23.8g total fat (8.2g saturated fat); 2412kJ (577 cal); 49.2g carbohydrate; 38.4g protein; 5.3g fibre

tips Blend or process any left over bread to make breadcrumbs. Freeze the crumbs, in user-friendly portions – they're incredibly useful to have on hand.
To save time, use roasted capsicum, available in jars from supermarkets and delicatessens, instead of roasting your own.

Menu Suggestion
starter Pear and witlof salad, page 105
dessert Blackberry parfait, page 109

Roasted beef fillet with horseradish mayonnaise

2 bunches fresh thyme
1kg piece beef eye fillet
2 tablespoons olive oil
1 teaspoon coarsely ground black pepper
1kg potatoes, cut into 3cm pieces
horseradish mayonnaise
2 egg yolks
2 tablespoons lemon juice
¾ cup (180ml) olive oil
1 tablespoon prepared horseradish
2 tablespoons finely chopped fresh chives

1 Preheat oven to 220°C/200°C fan-forced. Cover base of large shallow baking dish with the thyme.
2 Trim excess fat from beef; tie with kitchen string at 3cm intervals. Brush beef all over with a little of the oil, sprinkle with pepper. Cook beef in heated large frying pan until browned all over; place on thyme in baking dish.
3 Toss potato with remaining oil then place around beef; roast, uncovered, in oven, about 25 minutes or until beef is cooked as desired.

4 Meanwhile, make horseradish mayonnaise.
5 Remove beef from dish; discard thyme. Cover beef tightly with foil. Spread potato in single layer in baking dish; roast, uncovered, until golden and tender.
6 Slice beef thickly; serve with mayonnaise and potato.

horseradish mayonnaise Blend egg yolks and juice until smooth. With motor operating, add oil in a thin, steady stream until mayonnaise thickens. Add horseradish; blend until combined. Transfer to medium bowl; stir in chives. Adjust consistency by stirring in a little hot water. Cover; refrigerate until required.

prep & cook time 1 hour **serves** 6
nutritional count per serving 45.8g total fat (9.7g saturated fat); 2792kJ (668 cal); 22.6g carbohydrate; 40.4g protein; 3.5g fibre

serving idea Steamed baby peas.
tips Homemade mayonnaise is not hard to make, and it's well worth the effort, but if time is short, buy a good-quality whole-egg mayonnaise and flavour it to your taste with some lemon juice, prepared horseradish and finely chopped chives.
We used desiree potatoes, however, pontiac and sebago are also good. There is no need to peel them.

Main Courses Lamb

Rack of lamb with potato smash

½ cup firmly packed fresh flat-leaf
    parsley leaves
½ cup firmly packed fresh mint leaves
¼ cup loosely packed fresh oregano leaves
6 drained anchovy fillets, chopped coarsely
4 cloves garlic, chopped coarsely
⅓ cup (80ml) olive oil
6 x 3 french-trimmed lamb cutlet racks (900g)
1kg baby new potatoes, halved

1 Preheat oven to 200°C/180°C fan-forced.
2 Blend or process herbs, anchovy, garlic and half the oil until smooth. Place lamb in large, shallow baking dish; press herb mixture onto each rack.
3 Meanwhile, boil, steam or microwave potato until just tender; drain. Using fork, smash potato roughly in large bowl with remaining oil. Spread potato mixture on an oiled oven tray.
4 Roast lamb and potato, uncovered, about 20 minutes or until lamb is cooked as desired. Cover lamb; stand 10 minutes.
5 Increase temperature to 220°C/200°C fan-forced; roast potato, uncovered, about 10 minutes or until browned lightly. Serve lamb with potato.
prep & cook time 1 hour **serves** 6
nutritional count per serving 25.4g total fat (7.7g saturated fat); 1697kJ (406 cal); 22.2g carbohydrate; 20.5g protein; 4.2g fibre

serving idea Steamed green beans.
tip Make the herb mixture up to 8 hours ahead; keep the mixture with its surface covered, in the fridge. The rest of the meal preparation can then be at the last minute.

Menu Suggestion
starter Warm orange and fennel olives, page 105
dessert Caramelised apples, page 106

Spiced lamb roast with walnut & basil pesto

1½ tablespoons cumin seeds
8 cloves garlic, chopped coarsely
2 tablespoons olive oil
2kg leg of lamb, trimmed
500g piece pumpkin, cut into thin wedges
2 medium red onions (340g),
   cut into 6 wedges each
100g baby rocket leaves
2 tablespoons lemon juice

walnut & basil pesto
1½ cups firmly packed fresh basil leaves
½ cup (50g) roasted walnuts
2 cloves garlic, chopped coarsely
⅓ cup (80ml) olive oil
⅓ cup (25g) finely grated parmesan cheese

1 Preheat oven to 180°C/160°C fan-forced.
2 Dry-fry cumin in small frying pan, stirring, until fragrant. Using mortar and pestle, crush cumin, garlic and half the oil until mixture forms a paste.
3 Place lamb in large shallow baking dish; pierce several times with a sharp knife. Spread paste all over lamb, pressing firmly into cuts. Roast lamb, uncovered, about 1 hour 20 minutes or until cooked as desired.
4 Meanwhile, toss pumpkin and onion with remaining oil in large shallow baking dish; roast, uncovered, in single layer, for the last 20 minutes of lamb cooking time.
5 When lamb is cooked as desired, remove from oven. Cover lamb. Increase temperature to 220°C/200°C fan-forced, continue to roast pumpkin and onion, uncovered, about 10 minutes or until tender and browned lightly.
6 Meanwhile, make walnut & basil pesto.
7 Gently combine hot vegetables in large bowl with rocket and juice; serve with lamb and pesto.

walnut & basil pesto Blend or process basil, nuts and garlic until chopped finely. With motor operating, add oil in a thin, steady stream; process until mixture is smooth. Add cheese; blend until combined.

prep & cook time 2 hours **serves** 6
nutritional count per serving 39.3g total fat (10g saturated fat); 2654kJ (635 cal); 8.9g carbohydrate; 60.4g protein; 3.5g fibre

serving idea Accompany with crusty bread.
tip The lamb and vegetables can be prepared, ready for roasting, a day ahead of time.

Menu Suggestion

starter Crostini with fetta, artichokes and rocket, page 105
dessert Marsala-poached figs, page 106

Lamb cutlets with spinach skordalia

2 tablespoons olive oil
2 tablespoons lemon juice
2 cloves garlic, crushed
2 teaspoons dried oregano
18 french-trimmed small lamb cutlets (900g)
spinach skordalia
⅓ cup (80ml) water
¾ cup (50g) stale breadcrumbs
1kg spinach, trimmed, chopped coarsely
¾ cup (75g) roasted walnuts
2 cloves garlic, chopped coarsely
¼ cup (60ml) lemon juice
¼ cup (60ml) olive oil

1 Combine oil, juice, garlic and oregano with lamb in large bowl. Cover; refrigerate 1 hour.
2 Meanwhile, make spinach skordalia.
3 Cook lamb, in batches, on heated oiled grill plate (or grill or barbecue) until browned both sides and cooked as desired.
4 Serve cutlets with skordalia.

spinach skordalia Combine the water and breadcrumbs in small bowl. Drop spinach into large saucepan of boiling water; drain, rinse immediately under cold water, drain. Squeeze spinach to extract any excess water. Blend or process spinach and breadcrumb mixture with nuts, garlic and juice until smooth. With motor running, gradually add oil in a thin steady stream; process until skordalia thickens.

prep & cook time 30 minutes (+ refrigeration)
serves 6
nutritional count per serving 37.5g total fat (8.6g saturated fat); 1944kJ (465 cal); 7.7g carbohydrate; 22.3g protein; 6g fibre

serving idea Greek salad.
tip If you haven't much time, don't worry about the marinating – just brush both sides of the cutlets with the lemon mixture. In this case, make the skordalia first.

Menu Suggestion
starter Oregano-baked fetta, page 105
dessert Cherries with mint gremolata, page 110

Menu Suggestion
starter Fig and walnut roll with blue cheese, page 98
dessert Chocolate ice-cream with toffee-brittle, page 110

Barbecued soy & ginger lamb with coriander potatoes

1.5kg butterflied leg of lamb, trimmed
¾ cup (180ml) japanese soy sauce
½ cup (110g) firmly packed brown sugar
2 tablespoons olive oil
9cm piece fresh ginger (45g), grated
6 cloves garlic, crushed
⅓ cup (80ml) water

coriander potatoes
750g baby new potatoes, quartered
1 tablespoon olive oil
2 tablespoons finely chopped fresh coriander

1 Cut lamb into two even-sized pieces; combine in large shallow dish with sauce, sugar, oil, ginger and garlic. Cover; refrigerate 3 hours or overnight.

2 Drain lamb over small bowl; reserve marinade. Cook lamb on heated oiled barbecue over low heat, covered, about 30 minutes or until cooked as desired, turning halfway through cooking time. Cover, stand 10 minutes.

3 Meanwhile, make coriander potatoes.

4 Combine reserved marinade and the water in small saucepan; bring to the boil. Reduce heat; simmer, uncovered, 5 minutes. Strain into small jug. Serve sliced lamb with potato; drizzle with sauce.

coriander potatoes Boil, steam or microwave potato until tender; drain. Drizzle with oil; sprinkle with coriander.

prep & cook time 40 minutes (+ refrigeration)
serves 6
nutritional count per serving 19.5g total fat (5.8g saturated fat); 2140kJ (512 cal); 35.7g carbohydrate; 46.5g protein; 3.3g fibre

serving idea Steamed asparagus.
tip The flavour of the lamb will benefit greatly by marinating overnight; once that's done, the meal can be ready to serve in 40 minutes.

Slow-cooked lamb with white beans

1¼ cups (250g) dried cannellini beans
18 shallots (450g)
1 medium orange (240g), sliced thinly
3 cloves garlic, chopped coarsely
3 bay leaves
10 sprigs fresh thyme
½ teaspoon black peppercorns
1 bottle (750ml) dry red wine
2 x 1kg lamb shoulders
1 tablespoon olive oil
3 stalks celery (450g), trimmed,
    cut into 4cm lengths
⅓ cup (95g) tomato paste
800g piece pumpkin, trimmed,
    cut into 3cm cubes
½ cup finely chopped fresh flat-leaf parsley

1 Place beans in medium bowl, cover with water; stand overnight. Combine shallots, orange, garlic, bay leaves, thyme, peppercorns, wine and lamb in large dish. Cover; refrigerate overnight.
2 Rinse beans; drain. Place in large saucepan of boiling water; return to the boil. Reduce heat; simmer, uncovered, about 15 minutes or until beans are just tender.

3 Preheat oven to 160°C/140°C fan-forced.
4 Meanwhile, heat oil in large flameproof dish on stove top. Drain lamb, reserve marinade. Brown one lamb shoulder at a time in dish.
5 Add unstrained marinade to dish with celery and beans; bring to the boil. Add lamb to dish; transfer to oven. Cook, covered, about 2 hours or until lamb starts to fall from the bones. Remove lamb from dish; cover to keep warm.
6 Stir paste and pumpkin into dish, simmer, uncovered, on stove top about 15 minutes or until pumpkin is tender.
7 Serve sliced lamb with bean mixture; sprinkle with parsley and garnish with thinly sliced lemon rind.

prep & cook time 3 hours
(+ standing & refrigeration) **serves** 6
nutritional count per serving 26.6g total fat
(11g saturated fat); 2976kJ (712 cal);
29.8g carbohydrate; 61.5g protein; 12.3g fibre

tips We used golden french shallots, but brown pickling onions can be used instead. Instead of soaking the dried beans overnight, you can use 3 x 400g cans rinsed, drained cannellini beans, instead; add them to the dish after 1 hour of cooking time.
We found a bottle of shiraz worked well in this recipe.

Menu Suggestion
starter Fig, prosciutto and antipasti salad, page 102
dessert Affogato with frangelico, page 106

Menu Suggestion

starter Turkish bread fingers with good-quality extra virgin olive oil and dukkah for dipping
dessert Strawberries in rosewater syrup, page 113

Moroccan-spiced chunky lamb pies

2 tablespoons olive oil
2 medium red onions (340g),
    cut into thin wedges
4 cloves garlic, crushed
2 tablespoons plain flour
1 tablespoon ground cumin
2 teaspoons sweet paprika
2 teaspoons ground cinnamon
1.5kg trimmed diced lamb shoulder
1 litre (4 cups) chicken stock
400g can diced tomatoes
2 medium kumara (800g),
    cut into 2cm pieces
12 sheets fillo pastry
50g butter, melted
1 tablespoon icing sugar
¼ teaspoon ground cinnamon
2 teaspoons finely grated lemon rind
2 tablespoons lemon juice
1¼ cups (150g) seeded green olives, halved
½ cup finely chopped fresh coriander
¾ cup (200g) greek-style yogurt

1 Preheat oven to 160°C/140°C fan-forced.
2 Heat half the oil in large flameproof dish; cook onion, stirring, until softened. Add garlic; cook, stirring, until fragrant. Transfer to small bowl.
3 Combine flour, cumin, paprika and cinnamon in large bowl with lamb; shake off excess. Heat remaining oil in same dish; cook lamb, in batches, until browned.

4 Add stock and undrained tomatoes to same dish; bring to the boil, stirring. Return onion mixture and lamb to dish; bring to the boil. Cover dish, transfer to oven; cook lamb 1 hour. Add kumara; cook, uncovered, further 30 minutes or until tender.
5 Increase oven temperature to 200°C/180°C fan-forced.
6 Meanwhile, layer 6 sheets of fillo, brushing melted butter between each sheet; repeat with remaining fillo and most of the remaining butter. Using top of 2-cup (500ml) ovenproof dish as a guide, cut out 6 lids for pies, allowing about a 4cm overhang. Brush lids with any remaining butter; dust with combined icing sugar and cinnamon.
7 Skim surface of lamb mixture to remove any fat; stir in rind, juice, olives and coriander. Divide among six 2-cup (500ml) ovenproof dishes; top each dish with pastry round, folding in overhanging edge. Place dishes on oven tray; bake about 20 minutes. Serve pies with yogurt.
prep & cook time 2 hours (+ refrigeration)
serves 6
nutritional count per serving 39.5g total fat (17.7g saturated fat); 3336kJ (798 cal); 49.4g carbohydrate; 59.1g protein; 5.2g fibre

serving idea Balsamic-dressed mixed baby salad leaves.
tip Make the filling a day or two before you need it, or, the filling can be made and frozen for up to three months. If the filling is frozen, thaw it in the fridge for 24 hours before using it. By the time the oven is heated, you'll have the pies ready to bake.

Menu Suggestion

starter Dolmades with minted yogurt and olives, page 98
dessert Ice-cream selection, page 113

Lamb and lentil salad

1½ cups (300g) french green lentils

750g lamb backstraps

1 tablespoon olive oil

2 teaspoons ground cumin

350g baby green beans, trimmed

1 small red onion (100g), sliced thinly

1 cup (110g) coarsely chopped roasted walnuts

2 cups firmly packed fresh flat-leaf
   parsley leaves

200g piece fetta cheese, crumbled

pomegranate dressing

⅓ cup (80ml) olive oil

2 tablespoons lemon juice

1 tablespoon pomegranate molasses

2 teaspoons brown sugar

1 Cook lentils in large saucepan of boiling water, uncovered, about 15 minutes or until tender; drain.

2 Meanwhile, make pomegranate dressing. Combine half the dressing with lentils in a large bowl.

3 Cook lamb on heated oiled grill plate (or grill or barbecue), brushing frequently with combined oil and cumin, until browned both sides and cooked as desired. Cover lamb; stand 5 minutes then slice thickly.

4 Boil, steam or microwave beans until tender; drain. Rinse under cold water; drain.

5 Add onion, nuts, parsley, cheese and remaining dressing to lentils; toss gently to combine. Serve lentil salad with sliced lamb.

pomegranate dressing Combine ingredients in screw-top jar; shake well.

prep & cook time 40 minutes **serves** 6

nutritional count per serving 41.3g total fat (10.2g saturated fat); 2880kJ (689 cal); 26.4g carbohydrate; 48.3g protein; 10.8g fibre

serving idea Accompany with a loaf of warm crusty bread.

tip Pomegranate molasses is available at Middle-Eastern food stores, specialty food shops and some delicatessens.

Pork cutlets with caramelised pear sauce

1 tablespoon olive oil
20g butter
6 x 180g french-trimmed pork cutlets
2 tablespoons brown sugar
3 medium pears (700g),
    cut crossways into 1.5cm-thick slices
¾ cup (180ml) dry white wine
1 cup (250ml) chicken stock
¼ cup coarsely chopped fresh sage

1 Heat oil and half the butter in large heavy-based frying pan; cook pork, in batches, until browned and cooked as desired. Cover to keep warm.
2 Stir sugar and remaining butter into pan; add pear. Cook about 5 minutes; remove from pan.
3 Add wine to pan; simmer, stirring, 2 minutes. Add stock to pan; simmer, uncovered, about 10 minutes or until liquid has reduced by half. Return pear to pan with sage; simmer until heated through. Serve pork with pear sauce.
prep & cook time 35 minutes **serves** 6
nutritional count per serving 18.6g total fat (6.6g saturated fat); 1488kJ (356 cal); 18.8g carbohydrate; 22.3g protein; 2.6g fibre

Menu Suggestion

starter Pitta crisps with eggplant dip, page 98
dessert Plums with creamy vanilla yogurt, page 113

serving idea Steamed baby green beans.
tip This is a last-minute recipe; make sure you have any vegetables ready to serve as soon as the pork and pears are ready.

Pork loin with spiced orange relish

1.5kg rolled loin of pork
2 tablespoons olive oil
1 tablespoon coarse cooking salt
500g spinach, trimmed, shredded finely
½ cup (70g) slivered almonds, roasted
1 tablespoon red wine vinegar
200g piece fetta cheese, crumbled
spiced orange relish
3 medium oranges (720g)
1 cup (220g) white sugar
1 cup (250ml) water
⅓ cup (80ml) cider vinegar
¾ teaspoon fennel seeds
5 cardamom pods, bruised
4 cloves
1 cinnamon stick

1 Make spiced orange relish.
2 Meanwhile, preheat oven to 220°C/200°C fan-forced.
3 Dry pork with absorbent paper. Rub pork with half the oil then salt; place in large shallow baking dish, seam-side down. Roast, uncovered, about 40 minutes or until the rind crackles.

4 Reduce oven temperature to 200°C/180°C fan-forced; roast pork, uncovered, about 30 minutes or until cooked. Cover pork loosely with foil.
5 Meanwhile, combine spinach in large bowl with nuts, vinegar, cheese and remaining oil. Serve sliced pork with salad and relish; drizzle with pan juices.
spiced orange relish Quarter unpeeled oranges; slice quarters thinly. Combine sugar, the water, vinegar and spices in medium heavy-based saucepan; cook, stirring, over heat until sugar dissolves. Bring to the boil; stir in orange. Reduce heat; simmer, stirring occasionally, about 1 hour or until rind is tender and relish has thickened. Cool.
prep & cook time 1½ hours **serves** 6
nutritional count per serving 40.7g total fat (13.1g saturated fat); 3449kJ (825 cal); 47.2g carbohydrate; 64.5g protein; 5.7g fibre

tips The relish can be made up to three weeks ahead; keep, covered, in the refrigerator. Return relish to room temperature before serving. This recipe makes about 1½ cups of relish – more than you need; store the remaining relish in the refrigerator for another use.
Ask the butcher to score the pork rind finely.

Menu Suggestion
starter Cheddar with spiced pear paste, page 101
dessert Caramelised apples, page 106

Menu Suggestion
starter Samosas with tamarind sauce, page 101
dessert Plums with creamy vanilla yogurt, page 113

Green pork curry

1 tablespoon peanut oil
6 baby eggplants (360g), sliced thinly
200g fresh shiitake mushrooms, trimmed
¼ cup (75g) green curry paste
400ml can coconut milk
1½ cups (375ml) chicken stock
2 x 10cm sticks fresh lemon grass (40g), bruised
5 kaffir lime leaves, torn
1kg pork fillets, sliced thinly
300g green beans, trimmed, halved
1 tablespoon fish sauce
3 teaspoons brown sugar
1 tablespoon lime juice
¼ cup firmly packed thai basil leaves

1 Heat oil in wok; stir-fry eggplant and mushrooms until tender. Add curry paste; stir until fragrant. Add coconut milk, stock, lemon grass and lime leaves; bring to the boil. Reduce heat; simmer, uncovered, 5 minutes.
2 Add pork, beans, sauce and sugar; return to the boil. Simmer, stirring, about 3 minutes or until pork is tender.
3 Remove wok from heat; stir in juice and basil.
prep & cook time 30 minutes **serves** 6
nutritional count per serving 24.2g total fat (14.2g saturated fat); 1659kJ (397 cal); 8.8g carbohydrate; 33.2g protein; 6.8g fibre

serving idea Steamed jasmine rice and lime wedges.
tips This is a last minute curry. By the time the rice is cooked, the curry should be ready to serve.

Menu Suggestion
starter Bruschetta with tomato, basil and capers, page 102
dessert Chocolates with hot chocolate shots, page 109

Creamy pumpkin, artichoke and prosciutto pasta

1.5kg butternut pumpkin, cut into 1.5cm pieces
500g short pasta
2 tablespoons olive oil
12 slices prosciutto (180g), chopped coarsely
300ml cream
300g drained marinated artichoke hearts,
    cut into thin wedges
200g baby spinach leaves
¾ cup firmly packed fresh flat-leaf
    parsley leaves
⅓ cup (25g) finely grated parmesan cheese

1 Boil, steam or microwave pumpkin until tender. Drain, cover to keep warm.
2 Meanwhile, cook pasta in large saucepan of boiling water until tender. Before draining, reserve ⅓ cup of the cooking liquid. Drain pasta; cover to keep warm.
3 Heat oil in same pan; cook prosciutto, stirring, until crisp. Add cream and reserved cooking liquid to pan; bring to the boil. Reduce heat, gently stir in pumpkin, pasta and artichoke; simmer until heated through. Remove from heat; stir in spinach and parsley. Serve sprinkled with cheese.
prep & cook time 30 minutes **serves** 6
nutritional count per serving 33g total fat (17.6g saturated fat); 2976kJ (712 cal); 75.2g carbohydrate; 24.5g protein; 8.4g fibre

tips We've used casarecci, short lengths of rolled and twisted pasta, but you can use any short pasta such as penne or rigatoni. You could use left over roast pumpkin in this recipe; reheat it in the microwave oven, then add it to the pasta as per step 3.

Pumpkin ravioli and roasted tomato salad

500g cherry tomatoes, halved
2 medium red onions (340g), halved, sliced thinly
1 teaspoon caster sugar
¼ cup (60ml) olive oil
1kg pumpkin ravioli
100g baby rocket leaves
150g small black olives, seeded
2 tablespoons rinsed, drained baby capers
2 tablespoons red wine vinegar

1 Preheat oven to 220°C/200°C fan-forced. Line oven tray with baking paper.
2 Place tomato and onion on tray in a single layer; sprinkle with sugar, drizzle with 1 tablespoon of the oil. Roast, uncovered, about 20 minutes.
3 Meanwhile, cook ravioli in large saucepan of boiling water until tender; drain, combine in large bowl with tomato, onion, rocket, olives and capers.
4 Drizzle salad with combined vinegar and remaining oil.

prep & cook time 30 minutes **serves** 6
nutritional count per serving 18g total fat (4.7g saturated fat); 1542kJ (369 cal); 35g carbohydrate; 14.3g protein; 5.2g fibre

serving idea Accompany with a warm loaf of crusty bread.
tip Roasting the tomatoes concentrates the flavour, which goes well with pumpkin. Serve the salad warm.

Menu Suggestion
starter Crostini with fetta, artichokes and rocket, page 105
dessert Scoops of purchased hazelnut gelato

Eggplant, haloumi and rocket pizza

1½ cups (225g) plain flour
1 teaspoon dried yeast
½ teaspoon salt
¾ cup (180ml) warm water
2 tablespoons olive oil
2 cloves garlic, crushed
¾ cup (195g) bottled tomato pasta sauce
2 small red onions (200g), cut into wedges
1 small eggplant (230g), sliced thinly
250g haloumi cheese, sliced thinly
¼ cup firmly packed fresh oregano leaves
60g rocket leaves

1 Combine flour, yeast and salt in medium bowl; gradually stir in the water and half the oil. Mix to a soft, sticky dough; turn onto floured surface, knead about 10 minutes or until smooth and elastic. Shape dough into ball; place in large oiled bowl. Cover bowl; stand in warm place about 1 hour or until dough doubles in size.
2 Preheat oven to 230°C/210°C fan-forced. Oil two oven trays.
3 Punch down dough; knead until smooth. Divide dough in half; roll each half on floured surface into two 23cm x 33cm rectangles. Place dough on trays; prick with fork, spread with combined garlic and pasta sauce. Stand in warm place 10 minutes.
4 Meanwhile, combine onion, eggplant and remaining oil in large bowl. Cook, in batches, on heated grill plate (or grill or barbecue) until browned on both sides.
5 Top pizza bases with onion and eggplant mixture, cheese and oregano. Bake, in oven, about 15 minutes or until crust is golden brown. Serve pizzas topped with rocket.

prep & cook time 40 minutes (+ standing)
serves 4
nutritional count per serving 21.2g total fat (8.3g saturated fat); 2065kJ (494 cal); 50.9g carbohydrate; 22.1g protein; 5.6g fibre

tip Making your own pizza bases is not difficult and it's rewarding, but, if time is short, buy the bases and use the topping ingredients we've suggested.

Menu Suggestion
starter Warm orange and fennel olives, page 105
dessert Blackberry parfait, page 109

Chickpea and vegetable gratin

2 tablespoons olive oil

1 large brown onion (200g), chopped finely

4 cloves garlic, crushed

½ teaspoon ground allspice

½ teaspoon chilli flakes

2 x 400g cans diced tomatoes

2 large red capsicums (700g)

2 medium eggplants (600g),
    cut into 5mm slices

3 medium zucchini (360g),
    cut into 5mm slices

2 x 400g cans chickpeas, rinsed, drained

½ cup coarsely chopped fresh flat-leaf parsley

⅓ cup coarsely chopped fresh basil

1 teaspoon fresh thyme leaves

1 teaspoon white sugar

1 cup (80g) finely grated parmesan cheese

1 Heat half the oil in medium saucepan; cook onion, stirring, until softened. Add garlic, allspice and chilli; cook, stirring, until fragrant. Add undrained tomatoes; simmer, uncovered, about 15 minutes or until sauce thickens slightly.

2 Meanwhile, quarter capsicums; discard seeds and membranes. Roast under preheated grill or in very hot oven, skin-side up, until skin blisters and blackens. Cover capsicum pieces with plastic or paper 5 minutes; peel away skin then cut capsicum into 3cm pieces.

3 Combine eggplant, zucchini and remaining oil in large bowl; place vegetables on two oven trays, grill both sides until tender.

4 Preheat oven to 200°C/180°C fan-forced.

5 Stir chickpeas, herbs and sugar into tomato sauce. Place half the combined capsicum, eggplant and zucchini in shallow 10-cup (2.5-litre) ovenproof dish; pour half the chickpea sauce over vegetables. Repeat layering; sprinkle with cheese. Cook, uncovered, about 20 minutes or until browned lightly.

prep & cook time 1 hour **serves** 6

nutritional count per serving 13.3g total fat (3.9g saturated fat); 1296kJ (310 cal); 26.4g carbohydrate; 15.8g protein; 11.2g fibre

Menu Suggestion

starter Pear and witlof salad, page 105

dessert Marsala-poached figs, page 106

tip You could also cook and serve this in individual ramekins. Use six 2-cup (500ml) ovenproof dishes instead of a 10-cup dish in step 5.

Menu Suggestion
starter Pitta crisps with eggplant dip, page 98
dessert Strawberries in rosewater syrup, page 113

Vegetable tagine with split peas

2 tablespoons olive oil
1 large red onion (300g), sliced thinly
¾ cup (150g) yellow split peas
2 cloves garlic, crushed
5cm piece fresh ginger (25g), grated
3 teaspoons ground coriander
2 teaspoons ground cumin
2 teaspoons sweet paprika
1 teaspoon caraway seeds
1 litre (4 cups) vegetable stock
400g can diced tomatoes
750g butternut pumpkin, cut into 2cm pieces
350g yellow patty pan squash, quartered
200g green beans, trimmed, halved widthways
½ cup (125ml) water
½ cup coarsely chopped fresh coriander

1 Heat oil in large saucepan; cook onion, stirring, until softened. Add peas, garlic, ginger, spices and seeds; cook, stirring, until fragrant.
2 Add stock and undrained tomatoes; bring to the boil. Reduce heat; simmer, uncovered, stirring occasionally, 15 minutes. Add pumpkin; simmer about 15 minutes or until peas are tender. Stir in squash, beans and the water, cover; cook about 5 minutes or until vegetables are tender. Serve tagine sprinkled with chopped coriander.

prep & cook time 1 hour **serves** 6
nutritional count per serving 8.3g total fat (1.6g saturated fat); 1070kJ (256 cal); 27.8g carbohydrate; 13.5g protein; 7.9g fibre

serving idea Accompany with thick yogurt flavoured with grated lemon rind.
tips Cook the tagine up to the stage where the split peas are tender (step 2), several hours ahead if you like. Prepare the vegetables ahead of time, ready to add to the tagine for the last cooking stage. This way you'll retain the colours of the vegetables.

Menu Suggestion
starter Warm orange and fennel olives, page 105
dessert Great coffee with panforte, page 113

Spinach and herb cannelloni

1kg spinach, trimmed, chopped coarsely
500g ricotta cheese
2 eggs
1½ cups (120g) coarsely grated
   parmesan cheese
¼ cup finely chopped fresh mint
3 teaspoons finely chopped fresh thyme
2 teaspoons finely chopped fresh rosemary
250g cannelloni tubes
creamy tomato sauce
1 tablespoon olive oil
1 medium brown onion (150g), chopped finely
4 cloves garlic, crushed
4 x 400g cans diced tomatoes
½ cup (125ml) cream
1 teaspoon white sugar

1 Make creamy tomato sauce.
2 Meanwhile, preheat oven to 180°C/160°C fan-forced.
3 Cook washed, drained (not dried) spinach in heated large saucepan, stirring, until wilted. Drain; when cool enough to handle, squeeze out excess moisture.
4 Combine spinach in large bowl with ricotta, eggs, ½ cup of the parmesan cheese and the herbs. Using a large piping bag, fill pasta with spinach mixture.

5 Spread a third of the sauce into shallow 25cm x 35cm ovenproof dish; top with pasta, in single layer, then top with remaining sauce. Cook, covered, in oven, 20 minutes. Uncover, sprinkle pasta with remaining parmesan; cook about 15 minutes or until pasta is tender and cheese is browned lightly.
creamy tomato sauce Heat oil in large saucepan; cook onion, stirring, until softened. Add garlic; cook, stirring, until fragrant. Add undrained tomatoes; bring to the boil. Reduce heat; simmer, uncovered, stirring occasionally, about 20 minutes or until sauce thickens slightly. Cool 10 minutes; blend or process sauce with cream and sugar until smooth.

prep & cook time 1 hour **serves** 6
nutritional count per serving 31g total fat (17.1g saturated fat); 2412kJ (577 cal); 41.8g carbohydrate; 28.7g protein; 8.3g fibre

serving idea tossed green salad.
tip The cannelloni can be prepared completely up to a day ahead, ready to go into the oven. Keep it covered in the refrigerator overnight.

Baked kumara gnocchi with garlic cream sauce

2 large kumara (1kg), chopped coarsely
4 small potatoes (480g), chopped coarsely
1½ cups (225g) plain flour
1 teaspoon ground nutmeg
½ cup (80g) roasted pine nuts
1 cup (80g) finely grated parmesan cheese
garlic cream sauce
600ml cream
2 cloves garlic, crushed

1 Preheat oven to 180°C/160°C fan-forced.
2 Roast kumara and potato, in single layer, on oiled oven tray about 1 hour or until vegetables are tender; cool.
3 Meanwhile, make garlic cream sauce.
4 Increase oven temperature to 200°C/180°C fan-forced. Lightly oil six 2-cup (500ml) ovenproof dishes.
5 Mash kumara and potato in large bowl until smooth; add sifted flour and nutmeg, stir to a soft, sticky dough.

6 Divide dough into quarters; flatten each quarter on floured surface to 1cm thickness. Cut 5cm rounds from dough; transfer gnocchi to tea-towel-lined tray. Reshape and cut rounds from any remaining dough until all dough is used.
7 Cook gnocchi, in four batches, in large saucepan of boiling water, about 3 minutes or until gnocchi float to the surface. Using slotted spoon, remove gnocchi from pan; divide gnocchi among dishes, top with sauce, pine nuts and cheese. Cook, in oven, about 15 minutes or until golden brown. To serve, top with a little extra finely grated parmesan cheese.
garlic cream sauce Combine cream and garlic in medium frying pan; bring to the boil. Reduce heat; simmer, uncovered, about 5 minutes or until thickened slightly.
prep & cook time 1¾ hours (+ cooling)
serves 6
nutritional count per serving 57.6g total fat (32g saturated fat); 3474kJ (831 cal); 59.4g carbohydrate; 17.2g protein; 5.9g fibre

serving idea Baby spinach salad.
tips We used desiree potatoes; pontiacs would also work well in the gnocchi.
Season the dough with salt and pepper if you like. You can make the gnocchi and leave it covered at room temperature for several hours ahead of cooking.

Menu Suggestion
starter Haloumi with lemon, oregano and olives, page 101
dessert Plums with creamy vanilla yogurt, page 113

Menu Suggestion
starter Samosas with tamarind sauce, page 101
dessert Caramelised apples, page 106

Lentil and vegetable curry

1 tablespoon olive oil
2 medium brown onions (300g),
  chopped coarsely
1¼ cups (250g) brown lentils
1.25 litres (5 cups) vegetable stock
2 small kumara (500g), cut into 2cm pieces
400g broccoli, cut into florets
2 red banana chillies (250g), chopped coarsely

curry paste
2 long green chillies, chopped coarsely
5 cloves garlic, chopped coarsely
8cm piece fresh ginger (40g), chopped coarsely
1 cup firmly packed fresh coriander leaves
1 tablespoon olive oil

1 Make curry paste.
2 Heat oil in large saucepan; cook onion, stirring, until softened. Stir in curry paste; cook, stirring, until fragrant.
3 Add lentils and stock to pan; bring to the boil. Reduce heat; simmer, uncovered, 10 minutes. Stir in kumara; simmer, covered, 10 minutes. Stir in broccoli and chilli; simmer, covered, about 5 minutes or until lentils and vegetables are tender.
curry paste Blend or process ingredients until almost smooth.

prep & cook time 45 minutes **serves** 6
nutritional count per serving 8.3g total fat (1.4g saturated fat); 1283kJ (307 cal); 32.9g carbohydrate; 18.7g protein; 12.4g fibre

serving idea Steamed basmati rice and coriander-infused yogurt.
tips This curry is at its best eaten just after making it – the vegetables will discolour and become mushy if the curry is made in advance. To save time, make the curry paste and chop the vegetables up to a day ahead.

Menu Suggestion
starter Samosas with tamarind sauce, page 101
dessert Fresh peaches with lemon and mint, page 109

Tofu and vegetable laksa

600g piece firm silken tofu
3 baby buk choy 500g
2 tablespoons vegetable oil
1.25 litres (5 cups) vegetable stock
2½ cups (625ml) coconut milk
300g snow peas, trimmed, halved
½ cup coarsely chopped fresh mint
250g rice vermicelli
2¼ cups (180g) bean sprouts
6 green onions, sliced thinly

curry paste

1 large brown onion (200g), chopped coarsely
4 cloves garlic, chopped coarsely
4cm piece fresh ginger (20g), chopped coarsely
2 x 10cm sticks fresh lemon grass (40g),
   sliced finely
25g raw unsalted macadamias,
   chopped coarsely
2 teaspoons ground coriander
1½ teaspoons ground cumin
1 tablespoon sambal oelek
2 tablespoons lemon juice

1 Make curry paste.

2 Cut tofu into 2cm cubes; drain on absorbent paper. Trim ends of buk choy, separate leaves and stems.

3 Heat oil in large saucepan; fry tofu, in batches, turning carefully, until browned lightly all over. Drain on absorbent paper.

4 Cook curry paste in same pan, stirring, until fragrant. Add stock and coconut milk to pan; bring to the boil. Add buk choy stems, reduce heat; simmer, stirring, 1 minute. Add buk choy leaves and snow peas; simmer 2 minutes. Stir in mint.

5 Meanwhile, place vermicelli in large heatproof bowl, cover with boiling water; stand until tender, drain. Divide noodles among serving bowls; ladle laksa into bowls, top with tofu, sprouts and onion. Accompany with lime wedges.

curry paste Blend or process ingredients until smooth.

prep & cook time 40 minutes (+ standing)
serves 6
nutritional count per serving 39.6g total fat (21.6g saturated fat); 2629kJ (629 cal); 41g carbohydrate; 23.4g protein; 9.2g fibre

Starters

Beetroot dip with grissini and olives

Scoop a 200g tub of beetroot dip into a small serving bowl; serve with about 200g of your favourite olives (seeded green olives seem to marry best with this dip), and a bundle of traditional grissini (plain breadsticks).
prep time 5 minutes **serves** 6

Dolmades with minted yogurt and olives

Stir 1 tablespoon finely chopped fresh mint and 2 crushed garlic cloves into a 200g tub of greek-style yogurt; transfer to a small serving bowl. Serve with dolmades (about 18) and about 150g seeded black olives (kalamatas are good).
prep time 5 minutes **serves** 6

Pitta crisps with eggplant dip

Using 200g plain pitta crisps, top each with a teaspoon of eggplant dip, half a roasted walnut and fresh mint leaves and serve on a platter. Drizzle with olive oil.
prep time 10 minutes **serves** 6
note For individual servings, divide 100g plain pitta crisps, 200g eggplant dip, ½ cup coarsely chopped roasted walnuts and ¼ cup fresh mint leaves among six small plates.

Fig and walnut roll with blue cheese

Slice half a 250g fig and walnut roll thinly; serve on a platter with 150g piece creamy blue cheese and 175g oatmeal crackers.
prep time 5 minutes **serves** 6
note Fig and walnut rolls are available from some delicatessens and gourmet food stores.

beetroot dip with grissini and olives

pitta crisps with eggplant dip

dolmades with minted yogurt and olives

fig and walnut roll with blue cheese

samosas with tamarind sauce

cheddar with spiced pear paste

pâté with port onion jam

haloumi with lemon, oregano and olives

Samosas with tamarind sauce

Preheat oven to 180°C/160°C fan-forced. Place 12 samosas on a baking-paper-lined oven tray; reheat about 15 minutes (longer if frozen). Meanwhile, combine ½ cup water, 2 tablespoons brown sugar, 2 tablespoons tamarind concentrate, 1 teaspoon ground cumin and 1 teaspoon grated fresh ginger in a small saucepan; simmer for 5 minutes. Serve hot sauce with samosas.

prep & cook time 20 minutes **serves** 6

tip Fresh samosas are sold in Indian food shops and delicatessens, frozen samosas can be found in most supermarkets.

Pâté with port onion jam

Heat 30g butter in a medium frying pan; add 3 thinly sliced red onions, 2 tablespoons each of brown sugar, red wine vinegar and port. Cook over medium heat about 15 minutes or until jam is thick; cool. Divide 100g packet mini toasts and about 200g pâté among six small plates and serve each with a dollop of jam.

prep & cook time 25 minutes **serves** 6

tip Use your favourite pâté; we like a duck with orange flavour best for this recipe.

Cheddar with spiced pear paste

Place 200g cheddar wedge on platter with 100g spiced pear paste, 100g roasted walnut halves and 300g lavash strips.

prep time 10 minutes **serves** 6

tips Use your favourite cheddar; we like a sharp-tasting aged cheese. Spiced pear paste can be bought in delicatessens and some supermarkets. Lavash is a flat, unleavened bread of Mediterranean origin; it is available in major supermarkets.

Haloumi with lemon, oregano and olives

Cut two 250g pieces of haloumi cheese into 12 slices each; place in a single layer in shallow dish. Pour over combined ¼ cup each of olive oil and lemon juice; stand 10 minutes. Heat about 1 tablespoon olive oil in large frying pan; cook drained haloumi slices until browned both sides (reserve lemon mixture). Remove pan from heat. Divide about 100g rocket leaves among serving plates; top each with four slices of cheese. Add reserved lemon mixture to pan with 1 tablespoon finely chopped fresh oregano and 100g small seeded black olives; stir until heated through. Spoon dressing over cheese.

prep & cook time 15 minutes **serves** 6

Bruschetta with tomato, basil and capers

Seed and finely dice 6 ripe tomatoes; combine in medium bowl with 2 tablespoons extra virgin olive oil, ¼ cup fresh baby basil leaves and 2 tablespoons rinsed, drained baby capers. Cut 500g loaf wood-fired bread into 12 slices; toast slices both sides on heated oiled grill plate (or grill or barbecue). Rub one side of each slice with the cut side of a garlic clove; place toast on platter, garlic-side up. Top toasts with tomato mixture; sprinkle with freshly ground black pepper and drizzle with extra olive oil.

prep & cook time 15 minutes **serves** 6

Fig, prosciutto and antipasti salad

Halve 6 ripe figs. Trim excess fat from 12 slices prosciutto; roughly cut each slice into 2 or 3 pieces. Divide figs and prosciutto among serving plates; serve with equal amounts of 40g rinsed, drained caperberries, 300g quartered marinated artichoke hearts and 250g fetta-stuffed baby red capsicum. Serve salad drizzled with combined 1 tablespoon balsamic vinegar and 1 tablespoon extra virgin olive oil, and fresh baby basil leaves.

prep time 15 minutes **serves** 6

Oysters with mirin and cucumber

Whisk 2 tablespoons mirin, 1 tablespoon salt-reduced soy sauce and 1 tablespoon lime juice in small bowl. Peel 1 lebanese cucumber randomly, halve lengthways; remove seeds, dice finely. Slice 3 green onions diagonally. Place 48 oysters on the half shell on serving platter or plates. Drizzle mirin dressing over oysters; sprinkle with cucumber, onion and freshly ground black pepper.

prep time 10 minutes **serves** 6

Fennel, pecan and parsley salad

Stir ½ cup coarsely chopped roasted pecans and 2 tablespoons olive oil in small frying pan, over low heat, about 5 minutes or until pecans are browned; cool. Stir in 1 tablespoon lemon juice. Slice 3 trimmed baby fennel bulbs and 2 trimmed celery stalks as thinly as possible (use a mandoline or V-slicer if you can). Combine nut mixture, fennel and celery in large bowl with 1 cup firmly packed fresh flat-leaf parsley leaves. Divide salad among serving plates; sprinkle with coarsely crumbled 100g piece fetta cheese.

prep & cook time 20 minutes **serves** 6

bruschetta with tomato, basil and capers

oysters with mirin and cucumber

fig, prosciutto and antipasti salad

fennel, pecan and parsley salad

oregano-baked fetta

crostini with fetta, artichokes and rocket

warm orange and fennel olives

pear and witlof salad

Oregano-baked fetta

Preheat oven to 200°C/180°C fan-forced. Place 200g piece fetta cheese in small ovenproof dish; sprinkle with 1 tablespoon extra virgin olive oil, 1 tablespoon coarsely chopped fresh oregano leaves, ¼ teaspoon sweet paprika and freshly ground black pepper. Bake, covered, about 10 minutes or until cheese is heated through. Serve fetta warm from dish, with a sliced french bread loaf and seeded black olives.

prep & cook time 15 minutes **serves** 6

Warm orange and fennel olives

Peel thin strips of rind from 1 orange. Combine rind with 400g mixed marinated seeded olives, ½ cup dry red wine, 1 teaspoon coarsely ground black pepper and ½ teaspoon fennel seeds in medium saucepan; bring to a simmer. Stand 10 minutes before serving warm.

prep & cook time 10 minutes **serves** 6

Crostini with fetta, artichokes and rocket

Preheat oven to 180°C/160°C fan-forced. To make crostini, slice 1 small french bread loaf into 8mm-thick rounds. Spray both sides with olive-oil spray; toast on oven tray. Rub one side of each crostini with cut side of garlic clove; place crostini on platter. Combine 30g baby rocket leaves with 1 teaspoon each of extra virgin olive oil and red wine vinegar in medium bowl. Cut each of five marinated drained artichoke hearts into six wedges each. Top crostini with rocket mixture, then artichokes; sprinkle with coarsely crumbled 100g piece fetta cheese and freshly ground black pepper.

prep & cook time 20 minutes **serves** 6
tip Ready-made crostini can be found in various flavours in most delicatessens and some supermarkets.

Pear and witlof salad

Combine 2 tablespoons olive oil, 1 tablespoon red wine vinegar, 1 teaspoon dijon mustard and 1 teaspoon brown sugar in screw-top jar; shake well. Trim and separate leaves of 6 small witlof. Discard stems from 350g watercress; quarter, core and thinly slice 2 small pears. Place witlof, watercress and pear in large bowl with 1 cup coarsely chopped roasted walnuts; add dressing, toss to combine. Divide salad among serving plates; sprinkle with coarsely crumbled 100g piece creamy blue cheese.

prep time 15 minutes **serves** 6

Desserts

Marsala-poached figs

Combine 1 cup water, ½ cup marsala and ½ cup caster sugar in medium saucepan; stir over low heat until sugar dissolves. Bring to the boil; add 18 dried figs. Reduce heat; simmer, uncovered, without stirring, about 30 minutes or until figs soften. Serve warm with mascarpone cheese and biscotti.

prep & cook time 35 minutes **serves** 6

Turkish delight sundae

Blend or process about 150g fresh or thawed frozen raspberries with 1 tablespoon icing sugar. Coarsely chop four 55g chocolate-coated turkish delight bars. Layer vanilla ice-cream, raspberry puree, turkish delight mixture and ½ cup unsalted, roasted, coarsely chopped pistachios in serving glasses.

prep time 10 minutes **serves** 6

Affogato with frangelico

Place ⅓ cup ground espresso coffee beans in coffee plunger; add 1½ cups boiling water, stand 4 minutes before plunging. Place 2 small scoops of vanilla (or french vanilla or panna-cotta-flavoured) ice-cream in each of 6 small heatproof glasses or coffee cups; pour 1 tablespoon Frangelico over each. Give the hot coffee to the guests to pour over the ice-cream.

prep time 10 minutes **serves** 6

tip Pour your favourite liqueur over the ice-cream; orange and/or chocolate flavours work well with the coffee.

Caramelised apples

Peel, quarter and core 6 large apples; cut each quarter into 3 wedges; mix in medium bowl with 1 tablespoon lemon juice. Melt 50g butter in large frying pan; cook apple with ⅓ cup firmly packed brown sugar, stirring occasionally, about 10 minutes or until apple is tender. Divide among serving bowls; sprinkle with ½ cup coarsely chopped roasted pecans. Serve with thick cream.

prep & cook time 25 minutes **serves** 6

marsala-poached figs

affogato with frangelico

turkish delight sundae

caramelised apples

honeyed bananas with lime

blackberry parfait

fresh peaches with lemon and mint

chocolates with hot chocolate shots

Honeyed bananas with lime

Peel 1cm-wide strips of rind from 2 limes. Combine rind in medium frying pan with 2 tablespoons lime juice and 2 tablespoons honey; stir over low heat until honey softens. Remove pan from heat; remove rind and shred finely. Slice 4 large bananas into the lime mixture, mix gently. Divide banana mixture among serving bowls, serve with scoops of vanilla ice-cream and shredded lime rind.
prep & cook time 10 minutes **serves** 6

Fresh peaches with lemon and mint

Halve and seed 6 medium peaches; cut into wedges into serving bowl. Sprinkle with ¼ cup loosely packed fresh baby mint leaves; drizzle with combined 2 tablespoons lemon juice and 1 tablespoon honey. Stand at room temperature for 30 minutes before serving with greek-style yogurt.
prep time 10 minutes (+ standing time) **serves** 6
tip Nectarines and plums would also work well with the flavours of mint, lemon and honey.

Blackberry parfait

Roughly mash 300g fresh blackberries in small bowl; drain and reserve about ¼ cup of juice. Beat 300ml thickened cream with ¼ cup sifted icing sugar in small bowl with electric mixer until soft peaks form; stir in ⅓ cup greek-style yogurt. Layer cream mixture, berries and about 100g coarsely crushed vanilla meringues in serving glasses; drizzle with reserved juice. Divide another 150g blackberries among the glasses.
prep time 10 minutes **serves** 6
tip Use any fresh berries you like in this recipe.

Chocolates with hot chocolate shots

Arrange a small selection of your favourite chocolates on serving plates. To make hot chocolate shots, place 100g finely chopped dark eating chocolate in medium heatproof jug. Combine ½ cup full-cream milk, ¼ cup cream and 1 tablespoon coffee liqueur in small saucepan; heat without boiling, pour over chocolate. Stand 1 minute; stir until smooth. Pour into espresso cups or shot glasses; serve with chocolates.
prep & cook time 10 minutes **serves** 6
tip If chocolate is not quite melted, return to saucepan and stir over low heat until melted.

Chocolate ice-cream with toffee-brittle

Refrigerate 230g peanut brittle until ready to serve dessert. Put brittle into a strong plastic bag and coarsely crush with a meat mallet or hammer. Sprinkle crushed brittle over the richest best-quality chocolate ice-cream you can find. Shave 100g good-quality dark eating chocolate over the brittle.

prep time 10 minutes **serves** 6

Roasted blueberries with brie

Preheat oven to 160°C/140°C fan-forced. Place wire rack on oven tray; cover with baking paper. Rinse 375g fresh blueberries under cold water; drain but don't dry completely. Toss in medium bowl with 1 tablespoon caster sugar; spread, in single layer, onto paper-lined rack. Cook, uncovered, about 45 minutes or until blueberries shrivel slightly. Serve warm with a 300g wedge of ripe brie and 150g almond bread.

prep & cook time 50 minutes **serves** 6

Middle-eastern tasting plate

Place 12 fresh dates, 6 pieces turkish delight and 6 small pieces of baklava on a serving plate. Serve with good strong coffee. *(See notes on making coffee page 113.)*

prep time 5 minutes **serves** 6

tip Buy greek or lebanese baklava from specialty shops, delicatessens or some coffee shops.

Cherries with mint gremolata

Combine ¾ cup caster sugar, 1½ cups water and 2 cinnamon sticks in small saucepan. Stir over heat until sugar dissolves; bring to the boil. Reduce heat; simmer syrup, uncovered, without stirring, 5 minutes. Discard cinnamon. Place 900g fresh cherries in large heatproof dish; add hot syrup, cool. Combine finely shredded rind from 2 lemons and 2 tablespoons finely shredded fresh mint in small bowl. Divide cherries, with a little of the syrup among serving bowls; sprinkle with mint gremolata. Serve with cream, if you like.

prep & cook time 15 minutes (+ cooling) **serves** 6

tip Instead of using fresh cherries, use two or three cans of cherries: heat the contents of the cans in medium saucepan with 2 cinnamon sticks. Cool before serving with the gremolata.

chocolate ice-cream with toffee-brittle

middle-eastern tasting plate

roasted blueberries with brie

cherries with mint gremolata

ice-cream selection

strawberries in rosewater syrup

great coffee with panforte

plums with creamy vanilla yogurt

Ice-cream selection

Buy and freeze a variety of individual tub servings of the best quality ice-cream you can find. Pile all the ice-cream tubs into a large serving bowl or tray, and take it to the table for guests to choose their own. Don't forget the tiny spoons. Or, simply buy the best quality gelato in whatever flavour you think suits the rest of the meal, when in doubt, buy lemon-flavoured gelato, it's probably the most popular of all.

Great coffee with panforte

Place ½ cup ground coffee beans in large coffee plunger; add 5 cups water that has almost reached boiling point. Stand coffee 4 minutes before plunging. Serve with 290g round of purchased panforte, cut into wedges and dusted with icing sugar.

prep time 5 minutes **serves** 6

Tips for making great coffee

• Use filtered water – the purer the water, the better the coffee.

• Keep coffee beans in an airtight container in a cool, dark, dry place; grind the beans just before using. Once the beans are ground, their flavourful oils start to dissipate.

• If you prefer strong coffee, select an appropriate roast rather than using larger amounts of coffee.

• Coffee tastes best when consumed no more than 15 minutes after it hits the water.

Strawberries in rosewater syrup

Combine ⅓ cup water and ¼ cup caster sugar in small saucepan; stir over heat until sugar dissolves. Remove from heat; stir in 2 teaspoons rosewater. Stir in 750g hulled and thickly sliced strawberries. Divide strawberry mixture among 6 serving dishes; sprinkle with ⅓ cup coarsely chopped roasted pistachios. Serve with mini meringues and/or vanilla ice-cream.

prep & cook time 10 minutes **serves** 6

Plums with creamy vanilla yogurt

Drain the juice from 2 x 825g cans whole plums into medium saucepan. Add 2 cinnamon sticks and 6 bruised cardamom pods to the pan; bring to the boil. Reduce heat, simmer, uncovered, 3 minutes. Remove from heat. Add plums to juice mixture; cover pan, stand 10 minutes before serving. Meanwhile, make creamy vanilla yogurt by splitting 1 vanilla bean in half lengthways; scrape seeds into a medium bowl, stir in ½ cup greek-style yogurt, ⅓ cup thick cream and 2 tablespoons sifted icing sugar. Spoon warm plums and a little of the juice into serving bowls; serve with yogurt.

prep & cook time 15 minutes **serves** 6

Glossary

ALLSPICE also known as jamaican pepper; or pimento. Tastes like a blend of cinnamon, clove and nutmeg – all spices.

ARBORIO RICE small, round-grain rice, well-suited to absorb a large amount of liquid; especially suitable for risottos.

ARTICHOKE HEARTS tender centre of the globe artichoke; purchased in brine, canned or in glass jars.

ASIAN GREENS, MIXED BABY a packaged mix of baby buk choy, choy sum, gai lan and water spinach. Available from asian grocers and selected supermarkets.

BACON RASHERS also known bacon slices.

BASIL an aromatic herb; there are many types, but the most commonly used is sweet, or common, basil.
thai has smallish leaves and a sweet licorice/aniseed taste. Available from asian grocers, greengrocers and selected supermarkets.

BEAN THREAD NOODLES also known as wun sen, cellophane or glass noodles; made from extruded mung bean paste. Soak to soften before use; using them deep-fried requires no pre-soaking.

BEANS
cannellini small white bean similar in appearance and flavour to great northern, navy or haricot beans.
green also known as french or string beans, although the tough string they once had has generally been bred out.
sprouts also known as bean shoots; tender new growths of assorted beans and seeds germinated for consumption as sprouts.

BEETROOT also known as red beets; a firm, round root vegetable.

BISCOTTI means 'twice baked'; very crunchy biscuits. Are traditionally made by baking biscuit dough in two long slabs, then cutting into slices and reheating to dry them out.

BREAD
ciabatta in Italian, the word means slipper, which is the traditional shape of this popular white bread with a crisp crust. Also available as rolls.
pitta also known as lebanese bread. This wheat-flour pocket bread is sold in large, flat pieces that separate into two thin rounds.
sourdough so-named, not because it's sour in taste, but because it's made by using a small amount of 'starter dough', which contains a yeast culture, mixed into flour and water. Part of the resulting dough is then saved to use as the starter dough next time.

BREADCRUMBS STALE one- or two-day-old bread made into crumbs by blending.

BUK CHOY, BABY also known as pak kat farang or shanghai bok choy; is much smaller and more tender than buk choy. Has a mildly acrid, distinctively appealing taste and is one of the most commonly used Asian greens.

BURGHUL also known as bulghur wheat; hulled steamed wheat kernels that, once dried, are crushed into various-sized grains.

BUTTER use salted or unsalted (sweet) butter; 125g is equal to one stick of butter.

BUTTERNUT PUMPKIN pear-shaped with golden skin and orange flesh.

CANNELLONI a wide tubular pasta, about 7-10cm in length, filled with meat or cheese.

CAPERS, BABY picked early, they are smaller, fuller-flavoured and more expensive than the full-size ones. Rinse well before using.

CAPERBERRIES fruit formed after the caper buds have flowered; caperberries are pickled, usually with the stalks intact.

CAPSICUM also known as bell pepper, or simply, pepper. Be sure to discard seeds and membranes before use.

CARDAMOM can be purchased in pod, seed or ground form. Has a distinctive, aromatic, sweetly rich flavour; one of the world's most expensive spices.

CHEESE
blue mould-treated cheeses mottled with blue veining. Varieties include firm and crumbly stilton types to mild, creamy brie-like cheeses.
brie often referred to as the 'queen of cheeses'. It is smooth with a bloomy white rind and a creamy centre that becomes runnier as it ripens.
fetta a crumbly goat- or sheep-milk cheese with a sharp, salty taste.
haloumi a firm, cream-coloured sheep-milk cheese matured in brine; somewhat like a minty, salty fetta in flavour. Haloumi can be grilled or fried, briefly, without breaking down.
mascarpone a buttery-rich, cream-like cheese made from cows milk. Ivory-coloured, soft and delicate, with the texture of softened butter.
mozzarella a soft, spun-curd cheese. It has a low melting point and a wonderfully elastic texture when heated, and is used to add texture rather than flavour.
parmesan also known as parmigiana; is a hard, grainy cows-milk cheese.
ricotta a sweet, moist cheese; the name for this soft, white, cows-milk cheese roughly translates as 'cooked again'. It's made from whey, a by-product of other cheese-making.

CHICKPEAS also called garbanzos, hummus or channa; an irregularly round, sandy-coloured legume.

CHILLI use rubber gloves when seeding and chopping fresh chillies as they can burn your skin. Removing seeds and membranes lessens the heat level.
banana also known as wax chillies or hungarian peppers; are almost as mild as capsicum but have a distinctively sweet sharpness to their taste. Sold in varying degrees of ripeness, they can be found in pale olive green, yellow and red varieties at greengrocers and supermarkets.
flakes dried deep-red, dehydrated chilli slices and whole seeds.
hot chilli powder the Asian variety, made from dried ground thai chillies, is the hottest.
long green any unripened chilli; also some particular varieties that are ripe when green, such as jalapeño, habanero or serrano.
long red available both fresh and dried; a generic term used for any moderately hot, long (about 6-8cm long), thin chilli.
thai red also known as 'scuds'; tiny, very hot and bright red in colour.

CHINESE COOKING WINE also known as hao hsing or chinese rice wine; made from fermented rice, wheat, sugar and salt with a 13.5 per cent alcohol content. Inexpensive and found in Asian food shops; if you can't find it, replace it with mirin or sherry.

COCONUT MILK the second pressing (less rich) of grated mature coconut flesh; available in cans and cartons.

CORIANDER when fresh is also known as pak chee, cilantro or chinese parsley; bright-green leafed herb with a pungent flavour. This herb almost always comes with its roots attached as both the stems and roots of coriander are used in Thai cooking. Wash the coriander under cold water, removing any dirt clinging to the roots; scrape the roots with a small flat knife to remove some of the outer fibrous skin. Chop coriander roots and stems together to obtain the amount specified. Also available ground or as seeds; these should not be substituted for the fresh herb, as the tastes are completely different.

CRÈME FRAÎCHE a mature, fermented cream having a slightly tangy, nutty flavour and velvety texture.

CUCUMBER
lebanese short, slender and thin-skinned. Probably the most popular variety because of its tender, edible skin, tiny, yielding seeds, and sweet, fresh and flavoursome taste.
telegraph long and green with ridges running down its entire length.

CUMIN also known as zeera or comino; has a spicy, nutty flavour. Available in seed form, or dried and ground.

CURRY LEAVES available fresh or dried and have a mild curry flavour; use like bay leaves.

CURRY PASTES
green the hottest of the traditional pastes; contains chilli, garlic, onion, lemon grass, spice, salt and galangal.
red probably the most popular curry paste; a medium heat blend of red chilli, garlic, salt, onion, spices and shrimp paste.

DOLMADES a Greek dish consisting of grape leaves stuffed with rice, meat, lentils, vegetables and seasonings. Available from delicatessens.

DUKKAH traditionally an Egyptian specialty made of roasted nuts, seeds and an array of aromatic spices.

EGGPLANT a purple-skinned vegetable also known as aubergine.
baby also known as finger or japanese eggplant; very small and slender so can be used without disgorging (salting to remove the bitter juices).

EGGS some recipes in this book may call for raw or barely cooked eggs; exercise caution if there is a salmonella problem in your area.

FENNEL a roundish, bulbous vegetable, about 8-12cm in diameter, with a mild licorice smell and taste. Has a large swollen base consisting of several overlapping broad stems, forming a very pale green to white, firm, crisp bulb. The bulb has a slightly sweet, anise flavour but the leaves (fronds) have a much stronger taste. Also the name given to dried seeds having a licorice flavour.

FILLO PASTRY also known as phyllo; tissue-thin pastry sheets purchased chilled or frozen.

FIVE-SPICE POWDER a fragrant mixture of ground cinnamon, cloves, star anise, sichuan pepper and fennel seeds. Also known as chinese five-spice.

FLAT-LEAF PARSLEY LEAVES also known as continental or italian parsley.

FLOUR, PLAIN an all-purpose flour, made from wheat.

FRANGELICO hazelnut-flavoured liqueur.

GALANGAL also known as ka; a rhizome that looks like ginger but is more dense and fibrous. It has a hot ginger-citrusy flavour and is used similarly to ginger and garlic. Substitute with fresh ginger if unavailable, although the flavour will not be the same.

GINGER
fresh also known as green or root ginger; the thick root of a tropical plant.

ground also known as powdered ginger; used as a flavouring in sweet dishes, but cannot be substituted for fresh ginger.

HERBS we specify when to use fresh or dried herbs in this book. Dried (not ground) herbs can be used in the proportion of one to four, ie, use 1 teaspoon dried herbs instead of 4 teaspoons (1 tablespoon) chopped fresh herbs.

HORSERADISH, PREPARED horseradish that is grated then bottled in salt and vinegar; is not the same as horseradish cream.

KAFFIR LIME LEAVES also known as bai magrood, look like they are two glossy dark green leaves joined end to end, forming a rounded hourglass shape. Sold fresh, dried or frozen, the dried leaves are less potent so double the number if using them as a substitute for fresh; a strip of fresh lime peel may be substituted for each kaffir lime leaf.

KITCHEN STRING made of a natural product, such as cotton or hemp, so that it neither affects the flavour of the food it's tied around nor melts when heated.

KUMARA Polynesian name of orange-fleshed sweet potato often confused with yam.

LASAGNE SHEETS, FRESH thinly rolled wide sheets of pasta; do not requiring par-boiling prior to being used in cooking.

LEMON GRASS a tall, clumping, lemon-smelling and -tasting, sharp-edged grass; the white lower part of each stem is chopped and used in Asian cooking.

LEMON THYME LEAVES a herb with a lemony scent, which is due to the high level of citral – an oil also found in lemon, orange, verbena and lemon grass – in its leaves. The citrus scent is enhanced by crushing the leaves in your hands before using the herb.

LENTILS (red, brown, yellow) dried pulses identified by and named after their colour.
french green also known as puy lentils; they were originally grown in the town of Puy in France, but are now grown locally. A small, dark-green, fast-cooking pulse having a clean, delicate flavour. They are great to cook with as they retain their firmness.

MARSALA a fortified wine to which additional alcohol has been added, most commonly in the form of brandy (a spirit distilled from wine).

MAYONNAISE a rich, creamy dressing made with egg yolks, vegetable oil, mustard, and vinegar or lemon juice. We prefer to use whole-egg mayonnaise in our recipes.

MINCE also known as ground meat, as in beef, veal, lamb, pork and chicken.

MUSHROOMS
button small, cultivated white mushrooms with a mild flavour.
shiitake, fresh also known as chinese black, forest or golden oak mushrooms; although cultivated, they have the earthiness and taste of wild mushrooms. Are large and meaty.
swiss brown also known as cremini or roman mushrooms; light brown mushrooms having a full-bodied flavour. Button or cup mushrooms can be substituted.

MUSTARD, DIJON also known as french mustard. Pale brown, creamy, distinctively flavoured, fairly mild mustard.

NUTMEG a very pungent spice ground from the dried nut of an evergreen tree native to Indonesia; it is available in ground form or you can grate your own with a fine grater.

OIL
olive made from ripened olives. Extra virgin and virgin are the best, while extra light or light refers to taste not fat levels.
peanut pressed from ground peanuts; most commonly used oil in Asian cooking because of its high smoke point (capacity to handle high heat without burning).
sesame made from roasted, crushed, white sesame seeds; a flavouring rather than a cooking medium.
vegetable sourced from plants rather than animal fats.

ONIONS
brown and white are interchangeable. Their pungent flesh adds flavour to a vast range of dishes.
green also known as scallion or, incorrectly, shallot; an immature onion picked before the bulb has formed, having a long, bright-green edible stalk.
red also known as spanish, red spanish or bermuda onion; a sweet-flavoured, large, purple-red onion.
shallots also called french shallots, golden shallots or eschalots; small, brown-skinned, elongated members of the onion family. Grows in tight clusters similar to garlic.
spring has narrow green-leafed tops and a sweet white bulb (larger than a green onion).

OREGANO a herb, also known as wild marjoram; has a woody stalk with clumps of tiny, dark green leaves that have a pungent, peppery flavour. Are used fresh or dried.

PALM SUGAR also known as nam tan pip, jaggery, jawa or gula melaka; made from the sap of the sugar palm tree. Light brown to black in colour and usually sold in rock-hard cakes. Brown sugar can be substituted.

PANCETTA an Italian bacon.

PANFORTE a dense, flat, Italian cake that contains fruits and nuts. Available from some delicatessens and gourmet food stores.

PAPRIKA ground dried red capsicum (bell pepper); can be sweet, hot, mild or smoked.

PEPPERCORNS
black picked when the berry is not quite ripe, then dried until it shrivels and the skin turns dark brown to black. It's the strongest flavoured of all the peppercorn varieties.
green soft, unripe berry of the pepper plant, usually sold packed in brine; has a distinctive piquant, fresh flavour.

PINE NUTS also known as pignoli; are not, in fact, nuts, but small, cream-coloured kernels from pine cones.

POMEGRANATE MOLASSES is thicker, browner and more concentrated in flavour than grenadine, the sweet, red pomegranate syrup used in cocktails. It is available at Middle-Eastern food stores, specialty food shops and better delicatessens.

POTATOES
baby new also known as chats; an early harvested potato with very thin skin.
kipfler small, finger-shaped potato having a nutty flavour.
pontiac large with red skin, deep eyes and white flesh; good grated, boiled and baked.
sebago oval, white skinned potato; good fried, mashed and baked.

PRESERVED LEMONS a North African specialty; lemons are quartered and preserved in salt and lemon juice or water. To use, remove and discard pulp, squeeze juice from rind, rinse rind well then slice. Sold in jars or in bulk at delicatessens; once opened, store preserved lemon in the refrigerator. Adds a rich, salty-sour flavour.

PROSCIUTTO cured, air-dried pressed ham.

RICE VERMICELLI also known as sen mee, mei fun or bee hoon; used throughout Asia in spring rolls and cold salads. Similar to bean thread noodles, only they're longer and made with rice flour instead of mung bean starch.

ROCKET LEAVES, BABY also known as wild rocket; a peppery-tasting green leaf that can be used similarly to baby spinach leaves.

ROSEWATER distilled from rose petals and used in the Middle East, North Africa and India to flavour desserts; don't confuse with rose essence, which is more concentrated. Available from Middle-Eastern food stores and some health-food shops.

SAFFRON THREADS available in strands or ground form; imparts a yellow-orange colour to food once infused. Quality varies greatly; should be stored in the freezer.

SAGE a herb with narrow, grey-green leaves; slightly bitter with a light musty mint aroma.

SAMBAL OELEK (also spelled ulek or olek) Indonesian in origin; a salty paste made from ground chillies and vinegar.

SAMOSA a common snack in countries such as India and Pakistan. It generally consists of a fried triangular-shaped pastry shell having a vegetable and cheese or meat stuffing.

SAUCE
chilli we use a hot Chinese variety made from red thai chillies. Use sparingly, increasing the quantity to suit your taste.
fish also called nam pla or nuoc nam; made from pulverised salted fermented fish, most often anchovies. Has a pungent smell and strong taste, so use sparingly.
japanese soy an all-purpose low-sodium soy sauce made with more wheat content than its Chinese counterparts.
oyster a rich, brown sauce made from oysters and their brine, cooked with salt and soy sauce, and thickened with starches.
tomato pasta, bottled a prepared sauce made from a blend of tomatoes, herbs and spices.

SEAFOOD
blue swimmer crabs also known as sand crabs or atlantic blue crabs.
clams a bivalve mollusc also known as vongole; we use a small ridge-shelled variety.
firm white fish fillets any boneless firm white fish fillet – blue eye, bream, swordfish, ling, whiting or sea perch are all good choices. Check for any small pieces of bone in the fillets and use tweezers to remove them.
mussels should be bought from a fish market where there is reliably fresh fish; they must be tightly closed when bought, indicating they are alive. Before cooking, scrub the shells with a strong brush and remove the beards; discard any shells that do not open after cooking. Varieties include black and green-lip.
prawns also known as shrimp. Varieties include, school, king, royal red, sydney harbour, tiger. Can be bought uncooked (green) or cooked, with or without shells.
salmon red-pink firm fleshed fish with few bones; has a moist delicate flavour.
whiting fillets (sand whiting) also known as silver whiting, summer whiting, king george whiting or trumpeter. Substitute with bream.

SPINACH also known as english spinach and, incorrectly, silver beet.

STAR ANISE a dried star-shaped fruit of a tree native to China; has an astringent aniseed or licorice flavour. Available whole and ground, it is an essential ingredient in five-spice powder.

STOCK available in cans, bottles or tetra packs. Stock cubes or powder can be used. As a guide, 1 teaspoon of stock powder or 1 small crumbled stock cube plus 1 cup of water will give a fairly strong stock.

SUMAC a purple-red, astringent spice ground from berries growing on shrubs that flourish wild around the Mediterranean; adds a tart, lemony flavour.

TAMARIND CONCENTRATE the commercial distillation of tamarind pulp into a condensed paste. Used straight from the container, with no soaking or straining required; can be diluted with water according to taste. Found in Asian grocery stores and major supermarkets.

TOFU also known as bean curd; made from crushed soya beans. Comes fresh as soft or firm. Silken refers to the method by which it is made – where it is strained through silk.

TURMERIC has as acrid aroma and pungent flavour. Adds a golden colour to dishes.

VANILLA BEAN dried long, thin pod from a tropical golden orchid; the tiny black seeds inside the bean imparts the vanilla flavour.

VINEGAR
balsamic made from the juice of Trebbiano grapes; is a deep rich brown colour with a sweet and sour flavour. Quality can be determined up to a point by price; use the most expensive balsamic sparingly.
cider (apple cider) made from fermented apples.
red wine based on fermented red wine.

WATERCRESS one of the cress family, a large group of peppery greens. Must be used as soon as possible after purchase, as they are highly perishable.

WITLOF also known as chicory or belgian endive; cigar-shaped, with tightly packed heads and pale, yellow-green tips. Has a delicately bitter flavour.

WOMBOK also known as petsai, or peking or chinese cabbage. Elongated in shape with pale green, crinkly leaves, this is the most common cabbage in South-East Asian cooking.

YELLOW PATTY PAN SQUASH also known as crookneck or custard marrow pumpkins; a round, slightly flat summer squash being yellow to pale-green in colour and having a scalloped edge.

ZUCCHINI also known as courgette.

Conversion chart

MEASURES

One Australian metric measuring cup holds approximately 250ml; one Australian metric tablespoon holds 20ml; one Australian metric teaspoon holds 5ml.

The difference between one country's measuring cups and another's is within a two- or three-teaspoon variance, and will not affect your cooking results. North America, New Zealand and the United Kingdom use a 15ml tablespoon.

All cup and spoon measurements are level. The most accurate way of measuring dry ingredients is to weigh them. When measuring liquids, use a clear glass or plastic jug with the metric markings.

We use large eggs with an average weight of 60g.

DRY MEASURES

METRIC	IMPERIAL
15g	½oz
30g	1oz
60g	2oz
90g	3oz
125g	4oz (¼lb)
155g	5oz
185g	6oz
220g	7oz
250g	8oz (½lb)
280g	9oz
315g	10oz
345g	11oz
375g	12oz (¾lb)
410g	13oz
440g	14oz
470g	15oz
500g	16oz (1lb)
750g	24oz (1½lb)
1kg	32oz (2lb)

LIQUID MEASURES

METRIC	IMPERIAL
30ml	1 fluid oz
60ml	2 fluid oz
100ml	3 fluid oz
125ml	4 fluid oz
150ml	5 fluid oz (¼ pint/1 gill)
190ml	6 fluid oz
250ml	8 fluid oz
300ml	10 fluid oz (½ pint)
500ml	16 fluid oz
600ml	20 fluid oz (1 pint)
1000ml (1 litre)	1¾ pints

LENGTH MEASURES

METRIC	IMPERIAL
3mm	⅛in
6mm	¼in
1cm	½in
2cm	¾in
2.5cm	1in
5cm	2in
6cm	2½in
8cm	3in
10cm	4in
13cm	5in
15cm	6in
18cm	7in
20cm	8in
23cm	9in
25cm	10in
28cm	11in
30cm	12in (1ft)

OVEN TEMPERATURES

These oven temperatures are only a guide for conventional ovens.
For fan-forced ovens, check the manufacturer's manual.

	°C (CELSIUS)	°F (FAHRENHEIT)	GAS MARK
Very slow	120	250	½
Slow	150	275-300	1-2
Moderately slow	160	325	3
Moderate	180	350-375	4-5
Moderately hot	200	400	6
Hot	220	425-450	7-8
Very hot	240	475	9

Index

If you like this cookbook, you'll love these...

These are just a small selection of titles available in
The Australian Women's Weekly range on sale at selected
newsagents, supermarkets or online at www.acpbooks.com.au

also available in bookstores...

TEST KITCHEN
Food director Pamela Clark
Test Kitchen manager Belinda Farlow
Food editor Karen Hammial
Associate food editor Alexandra Somerville
Home economist Anneka Manning
Nutritional information Belinda Farlow

ACP BOOKS
General manager Christine Whiston
Editorial director Susan Tomnay
Creative director & designer Hieu Chi Nguyen
Senior editor Wendy Bryant
Director of sales Brian Cearnes
Marketing manager Bridget Cody
Business analyst Rebecca Varela
Operations manager David Scotto
Production manager Victoria Jefferys
International rights enquiries Laura Bamford
lbamford@acpuk.com

ACP Books are published by ACP Magazines
a division of PBL Media Pty Limited
Group publisher, Women's lifestyle Pat Ingram
Director of sales, Women's lifestyle Lynette Phillips
Commercial manager, Women's lifestyle Seymour Cohen
Marketing director, Women's lifestyle Matthew Dominello
Public relations manager, Women's lifestyle Hannah Deveraux
Creative director, Events, Women's lifestyle Luke Bonnano
Research Director, Women's lifestyle Justin Stone
ACP Magazines, Chief Executive officer Scott Lorson
PBL Media, Chief Executive officer Ian Law

Produced by ACP Books, Sydney.
Published by ACP Books, a division of
ACP Magazines Ltd, 54 Park St, Sydney;
GPO Box 4088, Sydney, NSW 2001.
phone (02) 9282 8618 fax (02) 9267 9438.
acpbooks@acpmagazines.com.au
www.acpbooks.com.au
Printed by Dai Nippon in Korea.

Australia Distributed by Network Services,
phone +61 2 9282 8777 fax +61 2 9264 3278
networkweb@networkservicescompany.com.au
United Kingdom Distributed by Australian Consolidated Press (UK),
phone (01604) 642 200 fax (01604) 642 300
books@acpuk.com
New Zealand Distributed by Netlink
Distribution Company,
phone (9) 366 9966 ask@ndc.co.nz
South Africa Distributed by PSD Promotions,
phone (27 11) 392 6065/6/7
fax (27 11) 392 6079/80
orders@psdprom.co.za
Canada Distributed by Publishers Group Canada
phone (800) 663 5714 fax (800) 565 3770
service@raincoast.com

Title New entertaining: the Australian women's weekly / food director
Pamela Clark.
ISBN 978 186396 727 3 (pbk.)
Notes: Includes index.
Subjects: Cookery. Entertaining.
Other Authors/Contributors: Clark, Pamela.
Also Titled: Australian women's weekly.
Dewey Number: 642.4
© ACP Magazines Ltd 2008
ABN 18 053 273 546
This publication is copyright. No part of it may be reproduced or
transmitted in any form without the written permission of the publishers.

Scanpan cookware is used in the AWW Test Kitchen.
To order books,
phone 136 116 (within Australia).
Send recipe enquiries to:
askpamela@acpmagazines.com.au